From the Street to the Executive Suite:

Remixing Street Smarts and Life Lessons into Leadership Success

From the Street to the Executive Suite:

Remixing Street Smarts and Life Lessons into Leadership Success

Dr. Janice A. Armstrong

Copyright © 2013, Dr. Janice A. Armstrong

All rights reserved. No part of this book may be reproduced, stored, or transmitted by any means—whether auditory, graphic, mechanical, or electronic—without written permission of both publisher and author, except in the case of brief excerpts used in critical articles and reviews. Unauthorized reproduction of any part of this work is illegal and is punishable by law.

ISBN 978-0-578-11501-6

TABLE OF CONTENTS

Preface vii
Introduction xi
Chapter One: Street Etiquette 1
- Leadership: It's Child's Play 2
- Earning Your Street 'Cred' 19
- Don't Sleep on Your 'Peeps' 21
- Chapter One:Leader Lessons Learned 24
- Action Activity: "Leadership Contract: Protecting Your 'Hood'" 26

Chapter Two: The Street Light Rule 27
- I Dare You to Cross This Line! 31
- Guarding Your Grill 34
- Beyond the Limits 38
- Chapter Two: Leader Lessons Learned 42
- Action Activity: "'Guarding Your Grill': What's Blocking Your Progress?" 43

Chapter Three: Leadership In The Household 45
- Who is the H.P.I.C? 46
- Taking Charge versus Being in Charge 49
- Chapter Three: Leader Lessons Learned 59
- Action Activity: Becoming the Head Person in Charge (H.P.I.C.) 60

Chapter Four: Life of the Latch Key Kid 61
- Discovering Your Independence 64

- Unlocking Capabilities 67
- The Latch Key Leader 70
- Chapter Four: Leader Lessons Learned 74
- Action Activity: Equalizing Your Life 75

Chapter Five: Dating and Elevating 77
- Making the First Move.. 79
- First Impressions 84
- Stereotype versus My Type 85
- Chapter Five: Leader Lessons Learned............... 91
- Action Activity: "You've Got Skills!" 92

Chapter Six: Taking Action- A Useful Way to Plan Your Leadership Lifestyle (Action Plan Development) 93

Acknowledgments 103

Author Biography 107

Preface

As I write this book, I think about the many years that have gone by and how much I have accomplished; however, those accomplishments were only more fulfilling when I conquered the trials and challenges that preceded them, like graduating from college, starting a family, reaching major life milestones that accompanied lessons learned. I often wonder how this city girl has made it to a government position and still thriving, with a reputation of a strong work ethic and great ambition. There were times when I just didn't want to be bothered with the world. There were other times, though very seldom, thank God, when I didn't want to be a part of this world. I had no purpose, no desire to dream anymore and that is when I lost myself. I did all of the things an upstanding good girl was supposed to do, but surely I participated in a few inappropriate moments. I am not gloating about my shortcomings, but my life's progress was definitely a testament to several wake-up calls, perseverance, and love.

This book is not about my life's story but more about how I have applied experiences in my life to become who I am now. Have I reached my ultimate goal? No, but I am still working on it. Knowing my purpose, which is to help develop and improve the lives of others, is far more important than attaining the goals. My purpose is the reason I even have goals. Will I reach all of them? It's possible, but not promised; however, I am content with that. There will be challenges faced, unexpected barriers that arise, and those OMG (Oh My Gosh for the not so text savvy) moments that may cause me to change my goals altogether. The most important thing is to be prepared for change.

Changes challenge people to grow. Some people will have more life changes based on the years they have lived on Earth and the experiences they have encountered. This book helps you tap into those experiences in a way that can help you see a different perspective and the importance in each experience encountered.

We have these memories of growing up that can make us laugh or cry or angry, but what we may fail to realize is that every experience comes with a lesson. When we are faced with similar situations again, those OMG moments turn to Ah Ha moments; treasure every moment.

This book will help you with, what I will call, a momentary transition, using previous life events to help you to grow. I hope it will tap into memories that have brought enough joy to your life that you would not mind experiencing them again; or recall the most painful parts that can encourage you to move forward in another direction to avoid repeated agony. This book will bring a smile to your face, but I hope it forces you to reflect. The chapters ahead focus on life's lessons and translate them into leadership lessons, lessons that will allow you to grow personally and professionally. This is not a wealth-building book. However, if you are fortunate to get to your ultimate financial goal, having learned lessons from this book, then I am pleased in knowing that my approach to leadership played a part. I can't physically hold your hand as you pursue personal and professional leadership ambitions, but I offer you this leadership handbook. I hope you enjoy it and find much purpose in it. Let's take this journey together: From the Street to the Executive Suite. I'll keep it street and simple to gain success.

Introduction

Turning Street Smarts into Book Smart Leadership

As I researched the definition for the term street smart, I came across the following definition and stereotypical explanations:

> "The general definition of street smart is someone who is intelligent, has good common sense, knows how to handle bad situations, and has the skills necessary to function where they live (usually the ghetto or the streets). However, the term is usually used to contrast and compare with another term known as "book smart".
>
> The stereotype of a street-smart person is someone who is intelligent and knows how to handle important situations in the streets but is not as well educated academically. However, the stereotype of a book smart person is someone who is upper class and well educated but less knowledgeable when it comes to handling important situations faced in bad neighborhoods and lower-class city areas.
>
> The more extreme and negative stereotypes are that street smart people are unintelligent and incapable of achieving a higher education, while book smart people

are naive, easily manipulated, and have bad judgment in bad situations. Both stereotypes aren't always true and any semblance of them [is] only due to different lifestyles and experiences."[1]

I grew up in Baltimore City. It was made very popular when HBO chose it for the setting of its series *The Wire*. Yet, Baltimore is known for so much more than the show's drug and crime depictions. There is a wealth of history that speaks through the streets of Baltimore City. Wars and battles were fought in its waters, great music legends started their careers, Jada Pinkett and TuPac Shakur became best friends while attending the Baltimore School of the Arts, and Francis Scott Key was inspired to write the *Star Spangled Banner* by the raised American flag in Fort McHenry. This does not overshadow the crime that has been witnessed in my city, but there is crime in every major city, just different types with potentially negative and even grave consequences. However, I will not say that having the reputation of being the "Home of the Wire" is not such a bad thing. If you followed the show you would definitely see what people have defined as street smart.

The characters, in *The Wire,* pursued illegal business ventures with the desire to survive and a need for wealth; many achieved financial success, but the costs were huge as the audience saw in the show's final season. One thing that always perplexed me was when I would hear the characters say school wasn't for them, but they are using the complexities of chemistry to produce their product. What if the dude who chemically created crack and accurately measured heroin, straightened up his life and used those skills to find the cure for a currently incurable disease? Just imagine the other possibilities and money making opportunities street chemists could have as authors, workshop leaders, and public speakers in the medical profession.

My Daddy often told me that I needed to be street smart. I always equated it with just simple knowledge and common sense. Street smarts are created through experiences that books may not offer. A person with street smarts learns from his experiences outside of a formal instructional setting and uses them in any personal or professional format they choose. My experiences in Baltimore were not one-dimensional. I had fun times in the projects where my grandmother lived; I sat on the porch of my house on the Eastside, people watching and taking in the sights; I've fought battles in my neighborhood and in school; I have even seen a dead body covered in the alley outside of a club. I have had my share of encounters that enhanced my ability to think with street intellect. This helped me as I continued to pursue my career, even when I didn't know what that career was. Street smarts heightened my intuition, what felt right and what didn't. Can I say my intuition was always right? No, but 90% of the time, it was right on target.

From the Street to the Executive Suite will help build your intuition- to assist you with deciding what is right and best for you. It will serve as a guide to make you a better person by understanding that you may already have the tools needed for success. Street smarts, to me, is not limited to being in the mode of "survival of the fittest" (the fond words of Mobb Deep (and also Nas) for my street smart folks and Darwin for my book smart folks) and succeeding; they are the rules of our lifestyles that influenced our growth and development as people.

This book contains stories and experiences of my youth. I hope you are able to relate in some way or learn something new. It explores household structure, childhood experiences, street games, music, hip hop culture (all components of what I know as street smarts) and transforms them into lessons in leadership that can develop you personally and professionally. I attempt to mesh the two levels of smart - street and book, sandwiching them into one big Oreo of knowledge. I desire to educate all people at every level of experience. I hope that street smart people desire to read the book to expand their knowledge, and I hope the book smart people open their minds to a new way of thinking.

What I appreciate most is that I am definitely a better person because of the decision to be both street smart and book smart. Therefore, I encourage you to use your street smarts to gain simple knowledge toward ultimate success.

Chapter 1
Street Games and Fair Play (Street Etiquette)

The spoken and unspoken rules that help leaders gain respect in organizations

In recent years I have found that rolling (or driving) down a city street is like playing dodge ball with my truck, except I am the one avoiding any impact with a child or an adult who chills in the middle of the street. I remember playing outside when I was younger. Space was limited as my friends and I engaged in a game of freeze tag, kickball, hopscotch, or four square so we had to play in the middle of the street. However, I also recall that when a vehicle was coming down the street, someone would yell, "Car!" and our huddle would part like the Red Sea in order to let the car pass. It was a rule of play and a sign of respect to the driver because the street was the vehicle's territory and not ours.

I also remember how important it was, during game play, to be fair with the rules (spoken and unspoken). When someone wasn't playing fair or cheating, as we commonly labeled it, they heard about it in hopes that the level of remorse would become so intense that their apologies were sincere and their desire to change was evident. Does it sound harsh? Yeah, it does, but the lesson learned was more important. On a positive note, fair play made game play a whole lot easier. The winners won fair and square. For those who didn't win, it wasn't the end because another game on another day, he, she, or they had a chance to claim victory! Playing fair earned gamers respect, and others wanted to play with a fair player.

In leadership, we find that we are offered a field of play that gives us the opportunity to utilize, develop, or improve our skills. The games we used to play in our youth actually offer us leadership opportunities that we may not have known existed then, but can use to our advantage as adults. How can you gain and maintain respect as a leader? How can you make your environment fair for all who follow and/or work with you? Take a walk down memory lane, revert to your younger days and see how much you can use as an emerging or developing leader. Learn when to lead, how to effectively follow, and when to yell, "Car!" and get out of the way.

Leadership: It's Child's Play

Before we dive into your personal skills and attributes as an emerging leader, I want to help you understand leadership roles and follower support. Leaders are charged with the opportunities to lead many different types of followers. Think about a time when you created a team of individuals to accomplish a task. Now think about their behaviors. Ask yourself the following questions:

- Did they support your leadership?
- Were there challenges as you led?
- Did you find that your behavior as a leader and their behaviors as followers matched?

We don't always have the luxury of choosing with whom we work, but we can make adjustments as leaders to align with followers in order to effectively implement and execute tasks as collaborative and effective team members. Sigmund Freud, a guru in the field of psychology, stated that some of us cope with challenges by reverting to previous stages in our lives.[2] Allow me to guide you to your childhood stages, encouraging you to open your playful mind in order to engage your leadership skills that could assist your interaction with followers. Through this, you may find that leadership can be as easy as child's play.

Did you know that children's games were not created initially to cater solely to children? They were actually a way for workers to be trained in the work they had to perform. It enhanced their work skills for better implementation of work duties. Some examples include:

- **Hide and Seek:** this game was used for various occupations that involved gathering or catching livestock. Playing this game with coworkers allowed the workers to practice the skill of seeking out the animal and catching it. The game Tag serves a similar purpose as well.

- **Tug of War:** this game is played in many cultures, dating as early as the 9th century. In Gambia, Africa, where the game is known as *Crik Crak*, they used this game when hunting teams would disagree about which team would get the best pick of the captured animals. In Japan, they play *Tsunahiki* during the harvest time to predict which village will have the greatest harvest.

- **Hopscotch:** this game served as a leisure activity for Roman soldiers occupying the Great North Road in ancient Britain. The original boards were 100 feet long. The soldiers would use it as a boot camp activity. They would carry heavy loads in order to build strength, endurance, and agility.[3]

Young and old used games as pastime activities. They definitely worked hard to play hard. The playing hard benefited the elders because it kept them in shape. The physical activity helped them with endurance to work in their senior years. The games also groomed the little ones so that they could participate in the family work when they were old enough and learned enough to perform the duties. Furthermore, for children and teens that were old enough, games, as stated earlier, trained them to continue to get better at the work they performed.

I bet you didn't know that such games that we played on a regular basis had so much meaning prior to our learning them. There is a lot in life that can help us make sense of things to which we may or may not have been exposed. In this section, we will discuss leader and follower roles so that you can self-assess the leader or follower you desire to be or currently are. If you've played these games recently, in your adulthood, you can find greater meaning and application, yet still maintain the appreciation of how fun these games really are.

In order to help you understand leadership and leadership roles through game play, I will:

1) Explain the game and how it is played.
2) Describe the leader role that is represented in the game
3) Match a compatible follower that can make the relationship worthwhile
4) Provide an example of this type of leader to which you can relate

Get ready to reminisce and apply important concepts to your life.

Mother, May I...?

Mother, May I...? is played with one leader and several followers. The object of the game is for the followers to be the first person to step toward the leader in order to eventually become the new leader. However, the follower must gain favor with the leader in order to get into the leader's spot. The leader is allowed to face the followers or have his back turned away from the followers. The latter poses a greater challenge and can avoid any potential bias between leader and follower. With each of the followers' turn, the follower is allowed to request whether he or she can step forward and closer to the leader. They can ask to take a certain amount of baby steps, regular steps, or giant steps toward the leader. The leader maintains control by 1) rejecting or limiting the amount of steps taken and 2) deciding the type of steps the follower is allowed to take (e.g. baby steps, giant steps, etc.). The followers must bargain with the leader and negotiate steps taken, but again, the leader makes the final decision.

This type of leader is actually one who has full control. He or she makes the rules, decides to change them at any moment, and implements as he or she sees fit. This is called the despotic (or overbearing) ruler. The follower that would fit this type of leadership or ruling would be the fearful follower. This person, fearful of the outcomes of the leader's instruction, works to gain favor with the leader and follows the instructions to maintain that favor. The follower's gratification comes from survival---making it to the end by doing what was necessary, which is seeking favor from the self-gratifying leader.

Russell Simmons, the CEO of Def Jam Records and former CEO of Phat Farm Clothing, and author of *Do You* takes pride in being much like a Despotic Ruler. Not necessarily a bad thing as he wants to teach value lessons, which is wonderful. In order to be an intern for him, the applicant must complete tasks to prove his or her worth. The interns may request options that they feel will help them grow as an employee; however, the final decision lies with Mr. Simmons.[4] He determines what situations best fit to build the character and behavior of a potential employee. You may ask to take five steps; he may allow you to only take two and wait to take the other three. However, the follower, who may want the opportunity to work for him, will do as instructed.

The downside to this situation is that the follower may become frustrated, avoidant, or vengeful of the leader. As a leader, you will need to recognize changes in your follower's behavior and change roles accordingly to avoid a disastrous relationship. Eventually, the follower may seek different employment opportunities or his work will not support the organization.

Go Fish!

Go Fish! is a classic card game that involves requesting what is desired. Each player is given 5-7 cards to begin. The object of the game is to get 4 of a kind of any card by asking the other players if they have that card. If they do, they will provide the card the player has requested. If they do not, the requesting player will then be told to "Go Fish!" for the desired cards in the pot or deck of cards placed faced down on the table. The first player to match all of their cards wins.

With this concept in mind, *Go Fish!* explains what is known as the benevolent dictator. The leader has the ability to supply what he or she feels the follower needs to complete the task. Additionally, this is the person who gives up the necessary information as he or she is requested or dictates what the follower needs to do to attain what he/she desires. The benevolent (or considerate) dictator is knowledgeable of the job or tasks that need to be completed, but appreciates that authority of saying "Yay" or "Nay" to the follower's requests. However, this person does recognize the value in his followers; furthermore, benevolent dictators recognize the people's skills primarily for personal gain.

The laid back follower would most likely work with the benevolent dictator well. This type of follower is fine with doing what the job requires but with little effort. In order to avoid confrontation, the laid back follower will do what the benevolent dictator desires; the follower is straightforward, stating if he or she is able to complete the task or not. However, when the laid back follower realizes that he does have the ability to perform the task, the follower will perform it, just to be done with it. The follower will look to his peers for job fulfillment, but will complete the job duties to appease the leader. The follower will provide information only when requested, for the most part, much like the benevolent dictator would.

This type of relationship is individualistic, meaning that work is done primarily for one's own satisfaction and gain. For example, the leader's gain exists because the task will be completed. The follower's gain exists because he thinks about future benefits due to task participation and completion (i.e. "This needs to go on my resume!").

Simon Says

Simon Says is a game of instruction. It begins with one leader and several followers. The leader, or Simon, instructs the followers to perform a command (e.g. "Raise your hands" or "Stomp your feet") and the follower is supposed to follow the instructions only when the command is preceded by

"Simon Says..." If the followers perform the command without the leader saying "Simon Says," that follower is eliminated from the game. The last one standing is the winner.

The leader-follower relationship in this game is similar to that of the paternalistic clan chief and the rebellious follower. The goal of the clan chief is to look out for the entire clan, providing them with instruction that is in the best interest of the clan. The clan chief would like to see everyone work for the same cause and be successful, but that won't always be the case. Initially, a member may follow the instructions for the group, but may eventually become irritated with constantly following the group and may be rebellious at times; hence, the rebellious follower emerges. This is much like how a child may have initially listened and followed his or her parents' instruction, but only until the point where he or she feels grown and rebels.

In relation to the game *Simon Says*, the leader instructs the follower, which then becomes a test of loyalty, dedication, and stamina. However, the rebellion exists when, in some instances, the follower may intentionally be eliminated from the game because he may get tired or bored after some time. In essence, if the followers are not in agreement with the instructions given or the length of time it takes to succeed, they may bow out of the game on purpose. A follower may seek to remove himself from the situation to gain self-gratification, with little concern of the group's satisfaction.

So you may be thinking, "Can these people just get along?" The answer is yes. Despite the occasional rebellion, the parental advice is still accepted and respected. The follower may still possess the interests of the group; however, he may want to approach the outcome differently than instructed. The leaders seeks acceptance and appreciates being in the loop regardless of the follower's opinions of the matter.

What does this have to do with leadership or organizational development? Let's say there is a new project and you are instructing your staff (or followers) to participate. There is a staff member who understands what needs to be done and the vision you may have to achieve it, but he may not agree with how you are starting the project. The staffer suggests many alternatives to your instruction 1) because he does not agree and 2) he is seeking a way to work more effectively within his own skill set to achieve what the group desires.

Peter Piper

As much as I love Hip Hop and Run DMC's song, *Peter Piper*, this refers to the game, not the song. In the game, *Peter Piper*, the winner is determined by the person who can say the following statement the fastest and/or with the most precision:

"Peter Piper picked a peck of pickled peppers. If Peter Piper picked a peck of pickled peppers, then how many pickled peppers did Peter Piper pick?"

In the most basic form of game play, each player is allowed a chance to say the statement until it is determined who states it the best. This game can be played in different ways as well:

Multi-level game play: there are several groups playing this game simultaneously and the winners of each group go to the next levels to play other winners in the previous groups, until the winner is declared in the final group.

Visual wordplay: The words to the rhetoric are placed on the wall, out of order and the challenge is for the player to correctly recite the rhetoric while pointing at each word in order.

The democratic official is the leader type who will provide instruction for a task to the group. The group selects a leader from the existing members in the group with the skills to best complete the task; this may be a current leader or a follower. Once the leader is chosen, the group will follow the instructions of that person. Essentially, the followers will just go with the flow of things. The skilled workers are automatically supported if the group is comfortable with the fact that person can complete the task.

In organizations, this process is known as the 80/20 rule, where 80% of the work is completed by 20% of the people. The good part is that, as a leader, you are able to recognize the skills of your followers and attempt to create a sense of value in their work. However, the bad part can potentially cause burnout in your most skilled staff members if you overuse their abilities. As leaders, be sure to balance the skill set necessary for task completion among the entire team. The 20% may be most useful during implementation, but the other 80% of the people can still be trained in tasks that can assist so that 100% of the workers are contributing to 100% of the work.

Hangman

Hangman is a problem-solving game. The object is to figure out the leader's selected word for the game. The leader will create the hangman post without the stick figure man. Additionally, he will provide the topic to the followers so they have an idea of how to guess in order to determine the solution. The leader draws as many small horizontal lines on the board representing each letter of the word. The followers attempt to guess the letters until the word problem is solved. With each correct letter guessed, the leader will place the letter on the appropriate line. Additionally, the leader will keep track of incorrect letters guessed. With each incorrect guess, a part of the hanged man is drawn on the post, starting with the head and eventually ending with the feet. If the entire body is drawn because of incorrect letter guesses, the followers lose the game. If the word is guessed prior to hanging the man, then the game is won.

A situation relative to this game would occur with the absentee leader. The leader does not necessarily need to be present the entire game. He can just instruct another follower toward the desired answer. He can also post the word, begin the game, and leave the rest to the followers to figure out. The leader gives the instructions to the followers (or group) and asks them to figure out the solutions to the problem. The follower who best matches this type of leadership is the independent follower. Independent followers are okay with working without a leader. They are diligent about updating the leader with progress reports and other data in his absence. This type of leadership poses a mind-reader challenge; both the leader and follower work independent of each other with not much exchange of thought. Sometimes the absentee leader is not available enough to provide guidance and continued direction to meet the required goals. Consequently, the independent followers are not thoroughly instructed. Even though they appreciate the leader's absence, it may leave much to the imagination or many questions left unanswered that cannot be rapidly addressed because the leader is absent. The followers are left to read the mind of the leader while hoping to achieve the desired or intended goal(s) with the most accurate guesses to avoid being hanged.

Pin the Tail on the Donkey

Pin the Tail on the Donkey is a classic childhood party game. Like any party game, the winner gets a prize. In this game, the players are the followers and the game host is the leader. The object of the game is to pin the tail closest to the donkey's rear-end on the donkey board. Each player is offered a turn and the game host blind-folds them, spins them around, and places them in the direction of the donkey board. The challenge of being blindfolded and spinning the person causes the player's direction to be slightly distorted and possibly undetermined. The player who places the tail the closest to the target wins.

The game host is the transactional leader. This person is interested in two things: 1) getting the work done and 2) compensation. Long-term relationships are not of primary interest unless the follower performs to the leader's satisfaction. A matched follower for this type of leader is the follower with benefits. They desire to complete the task, no matter the duties or risks, if the price is right. Both leader and follower are self-serving; they both look forward to the end result and how it will benefit them.

In some instances, this represents the consultant-organization relationship. Leaders of organizations, despite having talents in-house, may seek consultants to get the work done. They go through the contracts process and secure the funds to pay consultants to complete the work. This is not necessarily a bad thing for in-house employees as the hiring of consultants can lessen the workload for all staff; however, it is also costly. The relationship is strictly about business, and the consultants come and go. This, in some respects, can actually show that leaders value their followers enough to get them help. There are people willing to do the work, especially if there are organizations willing to pay for it.

Mannequin Game

The goal of this game is not to crown a winner, but it is a game of trust. *Mannequin* allows the leader to move the follower in different positions while telling a story. This game is entertaining because the follower, who is not aware of the developments of the story, allows the leader to move them in many positions so that the leader's shaping can successfully execute the story.

In transformational (or change) leadership, the follower allows the leader to lead him or her more for the benefit of the organization than the follower. In comparison to the game the organization is the story; both needed successful implementation and completion during the change process. The transformational leader utilizes the four I's to execute change: Idealized influence (what makes the greatest impact on your leadership), Inspirational motivation (what gives you that extra boost to move forward), Individualized consideration (finding your individual skills to lead), and Intellectual stimulation (what powers your brain with new ideas for success). The follower appreciates the outcome that the four I's create.

Similar to the *Mannequin*, the follower knows that the leader's goal is to effectively tell the story. However, in order to do so, the leader needs the assistance of the follower and the follower is willing to trust the leader to perform the story. Similarly, the claymation-like follower is willing to be molded and shaped to help better the organization.

Follow-the-Leader

In the game *Follow-the-Leader*, the leader decides what gesture or move he will do and the followers mimic the move. This game can be played stationary and indoors or in motion and outdoors (i.e. following the leader while running, walking, and gesturing). The latter would require more energy and is potentially more difficult in play. In this case, the follower is willing to follow the leader and do as the leader does or instructs. During game play, the leader is expecting all followers to complete the series of movements. After everyone completes the series of movements or the course, a new leader is decided and that leader begins the game again with a different set of movements or course.

The servant leader focuses more on the follower than the organization. The leader takes time to lead the follower and performs duties in order to 1) teach the follower, 2) grow the follower, and most important, 3) lead the follower. The matched relationship would be that of the disciplined follower. This follower works to help the leader to achieve the vision. This works well since the leader is primarily preoccupied with the follower's growth than the organization's growth, yet the follower is loyal to implementing the leader's vision regardless. The disciple wants to be taught and has the choice to follow in the footsteps of the leader. The follower is disciplined in the skills he or she has learned from the leader.

In organizations, you may see a situation where a leader may receive a promotion, intends to leave the corporation, or plans to retire. This leader begins to teach a follower, of whom he or she trusts, to eventually perform the duties that the leader currently does. In the teaching process, the leader is grooming the follower in the tasks of leadership; in turn, the follower is willing to follow the lead. The follower will adopt the vision of the leader and will make every effort to accomplish the vision, not just because it needs to be done, but because of the loyalty, respect, and trust the follower has for that leader. Even though some duties may be difficult and challenging, the leader looks out for the best interest of the follower; similarly, the follower is willing to take the chances for the leader. The end state can result in the vocational growth of that follower.

Earning Your Street 'Cred'

Street credibility or street 'cred'[5] is a term used in urban areas that refers to the amount of respect a person, with a positive reputation, has in the city, on the streets or in the neighborhood.[6] The person commands a level of respect in a city environment due to experience in or knowledge of issues affecting those environments".[7]

In the inner city, if someone is witnessed working to improve the community, his street cred is pretty strong, and he is accepted. It is understandable that in the midst of the current financial crisis, many people wonder to whom they can turn and how problems can be solved. Martin Luther King, Jr. gained street cred because of the active stance he took for civil rights and racial equality. President Bill Clinton earned street cred in Harlem, NY because he decided to place his office there "to try to help promote economic opportunity in [his] own back yard…".[8]

The Street Credible Leader

As leaders, we should determine how we can best assist our followers, serving as role models to them. People need to know their roles and understand how they contribute to the greater purposes of the organization[9], or in this case, the community. To be street credible leaders, we need to utilize a values-based leadership that includes ethics, vision, and action.

Dr. King possessed charisma and sincerity, qualities that gained them trust and validation from the people he wanted to help or save.[10] Dr. King maintains street cred, even after his death. What legacy do you intend to leave based on the leadership you plan to provide?

Values and Ethical Leadership

As mentioned previously, values play a major part in role modeling; furthermore, it contributes to the development of ethical leadership. Ethical Leadership is when a leader exhibits core values in every aspect of his life in service of the common good. Dr. Bill Grace, founder of the center for Ethical Leadership, created the 4-V Model of Ethical Leadership.[11]

It focuses on the following:

- <u>Values</u> guide our choice making on all levels of our personal and civic lives.

- <u>Vision</u> allows us to frame our actions.

- <u>Voice</u> helps us articulate our vision in a convincing way that motivates them to action.

- <u>Virtue</u> shapes our behavior, striving to do what is right and good.

In urban communities, respect plays a major role in developing street cred. Leaders, who allow people to be themselves and approach followers with a sense of worth and value, show respect.[12] With ethical development, role modeling and the use of respect, leaders have the ability to implement change and effectively serve people in the community.

Think about your current level of credibility as an emerging leader. Is your work ethic and commitment commendable? Are your organizational values questioned? How can you grow from your current state? What needs to change? Remember, only YOU can make that change!

Don't Sleep on Your 'Peeps'

Growing up, you quickly realize who you can and cannot trust. You determine who has your back and who will turn their back on you. Establishing respect and developing a strong relationship over time will help strengthen the level of trust with your 'peeps' (or people) that is hard to break, unless there is a dramatic turn of events that makes one cautious about the future of the relationship. For me, I will trust a person until he gives me a reason to do otherwise. For example, as a friend, I would tell my friends secrets and entrust them with those secrets until they show me a reason why I shouldn't. As a wife, I trust the affairs of our household to my husband, and he hasn't shown me a reason why I would not be able to do that. As a supervisor, I entrust my team with the assignments given to them in hopes that their deadlines will be met. In most cases, I wasn't shown that they weren't doing what they were supposed to do.

Sometimes we have to decide of what things we need to take ownership and what things we can ask someone else to do. This can lessen the level of stress that can potentially arise if we try to do everything on our own. Did Stringer Bell do things on his own in HBO's *The Wire*? No. He had runners or in the corporate world, subordinates. Please note: BY NO MEANS am I supporting or condoning the illegal activity associated with Stringer Bell, but I can't ignore the fact that the same strategies used in this type of hustle made Notorious B.I.G. (RIP) and Jay-Z smart business men. What I do support is the fact that they, the rap artists, used the negative situation, transformed it, and turned it into a more positive future; a model that some of today's troubled youth can use and value.

When leaders and followers have a strong relationship, they are able to work almost effortlessly together. When they understand each other's dynamics, approaches, and work ethic, it makes utilizing the skill sets a whole lot easier. I remember discussing the career of Busta Rhymes, a talented rap artist in my opinion, with my husband. Busta wanted to be a member of the rap group, A Tribe Called Quest, as his group's style of rapping would, as he felt, compliment Tribe's sound. Although they were long-time friends, the members Tribe agreed and decided against the idea since Busta was still with his group,

Leaders of the New School (LONS). This left Busta Rhymes searching for a place to show his skill and talent, of which was undeniable. His boisterous, deep and robust voice graced the dynamics of the group, while his wild and crazy personality, at the time, meshed well. Because of the skill sets of both groups and the desire to create a song that would top charts, the group of friends, among both groups, collaborated on the *Scenario Remix,* of which, in my opinion, Busta Rhymes made a name for himself, hands down. His verse at the end of the song, that starts low, quiet and slow and explodes to attractive chaos, placed the staple in Busta's career that is now difficult to remove.

Busta Rhymes' brand of a rough, rugged, and eclectic rap style propelled him to five solo albums. He is now one of the most sought after collaboration artists in the industry, working previously with icons such as Janet Jackson and more recently, winning a Grammy from a collaboration done with Chris Brown and Li'l Wayne. We will never know if Tribe would have succeeded or not if they had allowed Busta to be a part of the group, but what we do know is that the industry slept on him, in my opinion. They saw him as part of a group and didn't initially embrace his individuality. He should have been solo from day one! He sought his own career path, even though, he trusted his friends to help him get to some relevant point in his career. After rapping with LONS and working on the collaboration, Tribe was awakened, even more when Busta was invited to create and perform a verse on *Scenario Remix*[13] of which he did not let anyone listen to until he got on the microphone to record. Everything happens for a reason. Busta learned where he fit musically. This only prompted him to desire more.

Leaders should not sleep on their followers. They should embrace the skills that the followers have to find a good fit for their talents, instead of having them seek it out on their own or placing them in positions just to put butts in seats. Leaders should serve as mentors for growth, as well as, pillars of strength for their followers. I am not saying that leaders should coddle their followers, but they should allow them enough space to learn lessons, be successful in their work, and trust that they will make the best decisions for themselves; furthermore, they should nourish those opportunities when they are presented.

Leader Lessons Learned

- True leaders know how to be effective followers.

- As leaders, have the desire to always do better. There is always room for growth.

- Understand different leader-follower relationships and recognize your type relative to a particular situation.

- Play fair! Be consistent with your followers and establish credibility and trust.

- Your values and work ethic shape your followers and support your organization; therefore, it makes a huge impact.

For the action activity, make a promise to yourself as to how you plan to lead your life. Determine the steps that you can take now and those you desire for your future. Don't let the plan go to waste. Share it with someone who is currently experiencing (or has experienced) similar ambitions and gain input and support from that person.

LEADERSHIP CONTRACT: PROTECTING YOUR 'HOOD

Instructions: Your life is your (neighbor) 'hood! You are in it every day. You learn from it on a regular basis. The encounters you experience can make you a stronger person. When someone enters your 'hood expect those who enter it to contribute to the improvement of your 'hood. How can your 'hood be a better place to live? Create the rules. Expect respect! Complete the following contract with your desires and wishes. Make it as long or as short as you like, but make it effective.

Street Etiquette: In order to make my 'hood a better place to live, I expect to behave in the following ways:
1.
2.
3.
4.

Game Play: The rules that must be followed are:
1.
2.
3.
4.

Street Cred: My idea of gaining respect in my 'hood includes:
1.
2.
3.
4.

Chapter 2
The Street Light Rule

The successes, risks, and costs of approaching and exceeding boundaries

Summers were always great when we were young: a long summer vacation, no homework (unless you were in summer school), more free time, and most important, more daylight (at least where I grew up). This allowed for more time to play outside and hang with friends. I would spend hours outside getting sweaty and dirty, and my pigtails would go in opposite directions, totally ruining the work my mommy put into my head the night before. My parents allowed us more independence to roam the neighborhood as we'd liked, under two conditions: 1) we were on the porch by the time the street lights came on and 2) if we weren't actually on the front porch, we had to be in earshot of their boisterous voices when they called for us.

    I used to go up an alleyway that connected our streets in order to go and play with my cousins and their friends; there were more kids to play with my age on their street, which was two blocks away. Daddy and my uncle had no problem calling us from the top or bottom of the alleyway because they knew we could hear them (Yeah, that's how loud my daddy could get and surely a telephone wouldn't have been a better option, right?). Once I was called, my uncle would walk me to the edge of the alley at the top of the hill and watch me walk to Daddy who waited two blocks down. This was the routine whenever I wanted to go and play. So I stuck to the rules...most of the time. Those other times, I "tested the waters", knowing and thinking, "I am here playing with my cousins. I can be late!" It wasn't until years later that my daddy wanted to teach me a sense of responsibility. He occasionally loosed my rope. When I couldn't handle the freedom, Daddy would eventually tighten the rope so I could choke and learn.

An example of this experience occurred when I tested my boundaries. I went up to my cousin's house when my parents weren't home. However, I left a note detailing my whereabouts. I knew Daddy had to pick up Mommy so I figured I had a bit more time before those streetlights came on. We had a running game of dodge ball going, and the sky was getting darker. Yet, it was light enough to see and still feel safe. I continued to play until Daddy called. We were down to the remaining victims. Surely, I couldn't leave at that point. Besides, it wasn't quite dark yet, even though the streetlight came on. I knew better, but kept playing. I heard him call again and again, but I ignored it. A few minutes later, he and Mommy came up the hill and they were furious: 1) because I didn't come when Daddy called and 2) they had to walk up that steep hill to get me. Boy, I got it THAT night, but I still had lessons to learn. I learned not to push my boundaries that day, but another incident made me question my boundaries. It was a choice between what was right and wrong.

A friend and I were making our way down the pathway, which was parallel to the usual alleyway. The streetlights started to come on. I was a block away from home when I saw an injured, stray dog. He was a mess, but had tags around his neck that displayed his contact information. He came over to us and my friend said that we should help the dog, who was yelping in pain at this point. I always wanted a dog and wanted to care for it, but I didn't know how. My friend stayed with her grandparents for the summer and couldn't take the dog to their house because her grandparents' dog was territorial. We were closer to her grandparents' house so she ran to get a rope to secure the dog. I decided to take the dog with me, even though my mommy hated dogs. I did, however, consider calling the number on the tag (cell phones didn't exist back then, so I had to trek it home). By that time, the lights were on, and I was nervous, but I really wanted to help the injured dog.

As I approached the house, I could see Daddy sitting on the porch. He got up and walked toward me with anger on his face. I walked toward him with sadness and fear on mine. He didn't yell at me because he was more curious about the dog. I told him that I knew that I was supposed to be home, but I saw the dog and felt that I needed to help it. Of course, our 'puppy dog' faces softened Daddy's heart and made him decide not to yell at me, but to help me. We called the owner, who lived on the block where the dog was found. He was missing for a week and no one bothered to help him. His owners were grateful. Just in case you are wondering, there was no monetary reward for returning him. There was something greater, a personal reward for doing, what I felt at the time, was right and in the best interest of the ailing dog. It was a risk worth taking in spite of crossing parental and physical boundaries.

Leaders must decide when it is appropriate to cross boundaries and when the outcomes may be worth the risk. At other times, leaders may feel the consequences of their mistakes when they deliberately push boundaries and the results, at times, can be detrimental. Yet, there are other times where pushing those boundaries and shifting gears a bit are well worth the risk(s) taken. Just be prepared for the pending outcome or consequences.

Think about situations in school, work, or growing up where the outcomes varied when you pushed the limits. How did it make you feel to do so? Was it worth the potential consequences that could have evolved from your decisions?

As we lead organizations, agencies, clubs, etc, we are faced with those decisions often; however, we should not attempt to always make those decisions alone. As you continue to grow as a respected leader, followers will help you when you decide to make risky decisions. Just be sure to communicate the potential outcomes of those efforts and make decisions that are in the best interest of your agency, club, or organization.

I Dare You to Cross the Line

I remember watching movies like *Breakin'* and *Beat Street* and learning the definition of turf or territory. There were crews that danced like their lives depended on it and left their mark on their opponents' turf, symbolizing success. However, there were times when crews just took it upon themselves to cross that invisible line into their opponents' turf to stake claim of what, they felt, was theirs. In *Breakin' 2*[14], ElectroRock, the opponents to TKO, had the nerve to break a window in the community center that was being refurbished, resulting in a chase. After being chased, ElectroRock led TKO and their crew under an overpass and, without saying a word, dared them to cross the line. Once TKO did, the challenge for a battle was set into motion.

Have you ever been dared to cross a line? In tag, if you were it, you couldn't cross into base or the safe zone. It is considered trespassing if you cross people's property lines.

It can be dangerous if an officer approaches you and tells you to stay put and you choose not to, as a matter of fact, that's just plain gutsy.

As mentioned in a previous story, I have faced instances of consequence and reward when I crossed the forbidden line. Sometimes it takes the guts to know when it is right to take those chances. Other times, people choose to cross lines because they desire to face the challenge presented and are curious about what will happen. Often times, the choice has benefits and other times it doesn't, but it is up to the person to truly decide what the greater outcome will be based on the decisions he makes. In *Breakin' 2,* TKO accepted the challenge and won, letting the ElectroRock dance crew know that they can't be stopped no matter the threat they posed. The underdog will either be rewarded or bit in the tail if it goes sniffing in the wrong territory.

Dogs are prime examples of the consequences of invaded space. At one time we had two dogs in our home. The younger dog would often dominate the older one and most times, the older one did not feel like defending herself, especially in the house. The older dog knew what we allowed in the house. We constantly had to separate the younger dog so that she would not become territorial and learned to share the space. When the older dog would go outside to have her private time, the younger dog would come trotting along with sly intentions. The older dog, since she was outside and had free reign to do whatever she wanted, would take that younger dog down. It was an environment where the older dog knew she could take charge and proved it every time the younger one dared to cross the line into her space. There are more extreme cases of crossing into territory that I see on court shows where a defendant states that his dog attacked a plaintiff's dog to stake claim to the territory and protect it even more so. So challenger beware!

In the workplace, we are faced with similar choices when we decide to cross the line with our supervisors and colleagues. When is the time right? Is it ever right? We have to have great intuition or a deep sense of when it is appropriate. As emerging or developing leaders, we learn when to be active, passive, assertive, or aggressive. We analyze which situations are unnecessary because approaching them will only take our energy verses acting on those times, assertively and possibly aggressively, to gain the desired outcome.

The biggest challenge in the workplace is crossing the line with supervisors. For various reasons, employees cower to the supervisor because the supervisor may aggressively prove that he or she is right. Employees are afraid to get low performance ratings or lose their jobs if they challenge their supervisor's actions, ideas, or behaviors. Are those threats and feelings real? Of course they are, but the good news is that it does not always happen. Some supervisors are very approachable; however, it is still up to the employee to determine the best way to approach uncomfortable situations or challenges.

Telling a supervisor "off" or "about themselves" surely is not the way and will only create an environment of defense. You aren't just crossing the line; you are pouncing on the person. One thing the professors drilled into our heads in counseling psychology courses was to remember to address the behavior, not the person. Assertively tell the supervisor how you felt about the actions that were done, not the type of person you feel they are because of the action. This will make the situation of confrontation more meaningful and less emotional. Will you always get what you want? Possibly not, but you will get an opportunity to discuss the matter at hand. In most cases, we desire to be heard not necessarily have our problems solved. The latter may take more time or possibly have no solution.

Guard Your Grill

My Daddy and I would watch boxing matches and he would say, "Whenever you have to fight somebody, just make sure you guard your grill!" He meant to protect my face, especially my mouth. He would add, "You don't want anyone to knock out your teeth!" I would think, "So getting punched in the eyeball is okay?" However, I understood what he meant. Many knock-outs occur with an unexpected punch to the jaw. The nerves are very sensitive so the recovery is not one that can happen immediately unless you are a pro and are used to getting hit there. Keep in mind that most of us who have occasional neighborhood squabbles are not pros.

When approaching a fight, know that the grill isn't the only thing you have to protect; you have to guard your entire body! Any open area is vulnerable to an attack, and you don't want to be caught off guard when that situation arises. Those exposed areas, if left unprotected, will experience the wrath of the opponent's blow. Predict the opponent's actions in order to determine his counteractions. As discussed previously, leaders will face challenges and will need to be prepared to address those unpredictable situations; otherwise the leader is left vulnerable and, in some cases, may lack credibility. Success in this area comes with experience and making a mental note of what worked and what didn't.

Each time I get in front of a classroom of students, I am extremely vulnerable. I have to make sure I am a step ahead of them. The moment I would take a step backward, I would be immediately tested as to what I knew and how I could help them. Becoming a professor at a fairly young age was never an issue; however, teaching my peers, ranging from 17 – 57 years old, was indeed intimidating at first. I had to put myself in their shoes often to ensure that I could relate to the situations in which they were dealing: being parents, full-time workers, first-time college students, etc. These students had very demanding lifestyles and decided to pursue their collegiate aspirations. Furthermore, they were investing in their education, of which, for their general psychology class, I was solely responsible.

I remember being so nervous the day before class started. All of my paperwork was ready to be disseminated and my opening speech was drafted; however, I just didn't feel comfortable. I wanted to ensure that the students knew I could teach them. As I worked my full-time gig, I had an epiphany: I decided not to be the cookie cutter professor. I was not going to enter the room, papers in hand, and deliver the welcome speech that would not guarantee any connection to my students. My first day would not be as dry as some the ones I experienced in undergraduate school. I was setting myself up for failure. How I started the class would set the tone for the next 15 weeks. I had to make an impact. I changed my game plan.

I decided to pose as a student. I walked into the room, dressed in jeans, a t-shirt, and sneakers and sat in the front row. I laid my book bag down and waited for students to come in. I watched each one: some were excited; some were tired; and some were scared. It was funny to witness. They waited for the teacher to arrive and in the meantime, I decided to tell them that I had this teacher before and failed because she was so hard. They were panic-stricken. The class started at 6pm; the time was 6:10pm. Students were growing antsy wondering if they had the right day and classroom. They began to talk amongst themselves and mumble subtle rants of frustration. At that point, I jumped up, walked to the podium and said, "Good morning class. Welcome to Psychology 101. I am Professor Armstrong," and I smiled. They grew silent and dazed and then laughed hysterically.

My approach was well received and actually made them feel comfortable. I, too, felt a sense of relief and comfort, allowing me to continue with the class with confidence. I earned my credibility and reputation as a down to earth professor who could relate to my students. They were open to listening to whatever I said for the rest of the semester. Were there challenges with my teaching? Of course, there were, but the level of comfort developed in my class allowed me to be honest with them and simply say, "I don't know," and reiterate that I was learning as well. If that rapport was not established early in our teaching relationship, those students would have had no problem challenging my intellect and authority. Even though my approach was to stay steps ahead, we faced that semester, with first time experiences, together.

Leaders should be prepared for any direction a new encounter may take, within means. Good leaders find alternative ways to handle a situation because there are often instances where things do not go as planned and you have to shift gears. Advanced planning would be ideal to combat potential situations that may throw the leader off balance, but that type of planning is not always available. A boxer may have studied his opponent's previous fights, recognizing areas of potential weakness, but what if that opponent trained well enough to recognize his or her own vulnerabilities and corrected them prior to the bout? A change in technique and approach would be critical if the boxer desires to win. As an emerging leader, last minute changes to your game plan may be the answer in order to avoid potentially hostile or challenging situations. Leaders have to stay on their toes, assess the current situation, and work to stay one step ahead or rise above it with tact, skill, and delivery. Be a prepared leader; take your stance, guard your grill, and claim victory!

Beyond the Limits

Earlier I mentioned the story when I crossed boundaries to do what I felt was right. Of course, I didn't know how my daddy would have accepted that decision, but that was the risk I had taken. As emerging leaders you have to assess the risks and benefits of any situation. When you walked the streets or the alleyways in your neighborhood and you saw the *Beware of Dog* sign, did you make the attempt to walk past the house despite the sign or find another way around to avoid being seen by the potential man killing canine? I remember when I was young and I would frequent an alley as it made it easy to get from one street to the next. There was a gate that adorned the sign, *Beware of Dog,* and there was a pit bull mix (as he was tiny, but scary) that lived inside of the gate. As the pit bull pup began to grow and recognize his strength, he would bite the wooden gate, bit by bit, in an effort to escape and see what was beyond his boundaries. In order to continue my shorter walk through the street, I would continue to walk the path despite the fact that I noticed he was making his way through the gate. What was once a hole in the gate eventually became an open window for him to show his ugly head and bark, but I kept walking by the gate. The hole wasn't big enough for him to fit, so I didn't care.

Weeks later, as I walked from the store with my cousin, we made a horrible discovery. That ugly, mean dog stood outside of the gate while it was still closed. He managed to eat a doorway through it. Where were his owners while this happened? They were right there, in the house, watching the emergence of this doggy door that the canine created.

I was lucky because I was on the street where I lived so I didn't have to approach that mangy beast any further; however, my cousin, who lived at the top of the alley, had to make her way past him. Was she bold enough to take the usual path past him in hopes that he would do her no harm? Of course not! He bit into the wooden gate for God's sake!!

So she changed her plans and took the long way; I walked her halfway home in order to ensure her safety. We later notified the owners. They temporarily fixed the gate by covering it with another wooden board! Need I say more as to what happened to THAT one? I think you can imagine.

One day I challenged the mutt; I walked up the alleyway while he was standing there. I found out, at that moment, that he was all bark AND bite, but just not with me. I was not sure why, but when I approached the dog, he actually cowered and became quiet. I challenged his authority. That was crazy, right? Yes, it was, but how can a dog run an alleyway? If you give him the opportunity to become territorial, he will. But the alleyway wasn't just his territory; it was shared.

So why is this story important to leadership? Sometimes, in our workplace, we may encounter a colleague or a manager whose personality is much like the mangy mutt. They create a negative vibe to the workplace that puts everyone on edge. Not everyone will be positive, but it is up to you, as an emerging leader to attempt to sustain a positive attitude when faced with negativity. I am not saying that you can never get upset about a challenging situation; surely, you can, but you have the choice of when and where it is appropriate to vent those emotions. You will then be labeled as "the mangy mutt" if not done appropriately. Two mean mutts will only cause a dog fight.

In my past, I was approached with a difficult colleague. Not sure why she was difficult, but I never held it against her. She had a lot going on in her life that, unfortunately, bled in the workplace. Many were wondering why she brought this attitude to every situation possible in order to make things difficult; she openly admitted her tactics. I was cool with that, kept my distance most times, until the situation became personal, well more of a professional attack on me, in front of our supervisor. In short, I challenged her in front of our supervisor and asked her to confirm the truth. She did and later acknowledged that I pretty much "had balls." If anything, it made me see a different side of her, a more positive side, and I am happy to continue to witness her growth and happiness today in a personal capacity.

As leaders, we have to recognize the true meaning behind difficult employees. We need to show a level of compassion that indicates that we care about the work-life balance that needs to exist and to help employee's solve issues. We are the models who can affect employee attitudes and work ethic in our organizations. People often say that they don't develop friendships at the workplace. How can you not develop some form of relationship that involves some personal infusion when you are at your job 8-10 hours per day? Whether you actively introduce yourself or not, people, via interactions, will get to know you. It's intuitive; however, those intuitions can only be stapled through valid experiences. If I felt that my old coworker was always that type of person, then the challenge wouldn't have made a difference. I personally felt that challenging her would change her, giving her insight of how she treated others. Sometimes people don't see the error of their own ways, and those ways need to be pointed out, in a dignified way. Go beyond the limits of what you witness and, as a leader, try to get to the root cause of what may be plaguing your followers. It will create a kind kennel where all are comfortable. It will also benefit you and your followers in the long run.

Leader Lessons Learned

- When crossing boundaries, ensure that the benefits outweigh the risks. Bottom line: Will it be worth it?

- Accept the challenges that come with going beyond your limits.

- Learn to approach challenging situations with dignity and tact. Don't burn your bridges saying something you will regret later.

- When possible, create a back-up plan for potentially challenging situations. Preparation is key.

- Challenging peers and followers may be difficult to handle, but efficient leaders learn the best approach in order to maintain a healthy environment for all.

GUARDING YOUR GRILL:

WHAT'S BLOCKING YOUR PROGRESS?

Instructions: Many of us desire to be the best person we can be. We have dreams, goals and aspirations that we talk about, but want more to be about. Who is that person you want to become? How do you intend to get to that place? We can have these grand ideas, but actually putting them in writing not only provides an outlook of our future, but also creates a sense of accountability to strive to achieve. List your goals below and truly think about how you can achieve them. Write out the potential barriers that can hinder your success and ways that you can overcome those barriers. Also, create a timeline to achieve your goal(s). Guard your grill, combat what challenges you and create a plan for your success.

GOALS	POTENTIAL BARRIERS	STRATEGIES	TIMELINES
Ex: Submit college applications by (set a deadline)	Ex: Currently school project due Bad time management skills	Ex: Make note of the timelines and complete a little per day so it doesn't seem overwhelming.	Ex: Complete the task by the date on the application

Chapter 3

Leadership In The Household

How household regulations and roles translate into effective leadership skills

It was unwritten, between my siblings and I, that Daddy and Mommy were the heads of the household. When one parent was absent the responsibilities of the other were solely executed. Furthermore, when my parents were not home, the roles and responsibilities were given to the oldest in the house or the person who they left in charge. Whether it was our parents, my neighbors, my grandma, my older sister, or whoever, we gave respect to the person left in charge. Now I can honestly say that I challenged my sister and any older cousins left in charge of me when I was younger and in turn, my little brother challenged me as well. We understood the chain of command, but through experiences I can't say that I saw my older sister being the boss or in charge. However, she took her role seriously, as I did with my younger brother. Yet, I felt that respect still needed to be earned when cousins and siblings were left in charge, but we never questioned our level of respect when adults took care of us.

When my sister was left in charge, she was not allowed to scold me or punish me, but to report any disrespectful and unacceptable actions to my parents and they handled me as they saw fit. Sometimes my sister ignored that rule, as I also did with my brother, and a few physical encounters occurred (typical sibling rivalry, you know); however, we ALL got scolded for that!

When the heads of households decide to leave their homes in the care of someone else, the selection process is based on prior leadership experiences to determine if the potential leader is responsible to take action; however, there are rules of that particular household that need to be obeyed and remain consistent so that the structure of the household is not significantly changed by the temporary lead. Let us explore the different roles, responsibilities and structures of the household and how developing a functional and solid household can influence your leadership responsibilities of building a solid organization.

Who's the Head Person in Charge (H.P.I.C)?

This approach to leadership in the household models what is seen more often than not in the workplace. There is a four-generation mix in today's organizations and, even based on my own experiences, younger persons in leadership positions are questioned by more seasoned individuals. It isn't that young leaders cannot do the work, but more of the perception that "youth" means lack of experience, which is not necessarily so, but generally accepted as such. Young leaders have to prove their worth, experience, and knowledge to achieve and maintain positions of leadership. What are the pros and cons of having a young leader in position of power? A con is that it can add undue stress on the leader in some workplace situations; however, a pro is that once skills are proven, young leaders are accepted into the fold. Is it a form of proving yourself worthy to be a part of an unidentified leadership fraternity? Yes indeed!

On the other hand, there are older employees, from the Baby Boom era, who desire to work longer in their careers and have to prove worthy to stay on the job. For example, the "Original Gangsta" (or "OG") has been at his job for a while and knows the ins and outs of what is required long before a "young cat" comes in, with new experiences, attempting to change the game. Innovation and creativity is embraced in leadership, but not always accepted. Sometimes, depending on the experiences of the employee, he would like to leave well enough alone, keeping things as they are; however, the constant innovation in most industries requires taking the next steps in order to remain competitive to customers. If anything, no matter your age and experience, embrace this opportunity to show your worth and be open to learning new things. If you are complacent or just simply satisfied with your current status, with no flexibility to grow, then frankly, leadership, at any level, is not for you.

This holds true with presidents of high school and collegiate organizations. The president of the Student Government Association does not have to be a senior. If anything it is best that they still have time at their respective university to continue to offer input and influence; therefore, sophomores and juniors should not be ignored to take on leadership positions. Additionally, followers will continue to look for fresh, new, and interesting ideas to enhance the club. A candidate who has the skill set to bring these ideas to the table may influence the vote in his favor.

When choosing the H.P.I.C, ensure that he is able to prove what the organization, agency, or club needs; otherwise, if he is set in that leadership position with little experience, determine what support network can help him spark innovation and creativity, temporarily or permanently. However, when pursuing all of these goals for leadership, it doesn't take away from the fact that the organization still needs to function and thrive as the senior leadership, CEOs or club advisors desire.

In my parents' absence, my sister or I may have done things differently and possibly even better than our parents. The ultimate concerns, however, were that the affairs of the house were in order, the house was still standing, and no one was hurt.

Taking Charge versus Being in Charge

Parents, who leave home for whatever reason, decide who is in charge of the household in their absence. Some of us may take on the responsibility, willingly, in order to prove that we can be responsible; some will avoid it so they won't be held accountable. Those who accept the challenge may even go overboard, owning responsibilities that aren't theirs (i.e. disciplining, delegating, etc). When Daddy and Mommy left either my sister or I in charge, our responsibilities were limited to feeding each other, ensuring homework was complete, and overseeing assigned tasks. On many occasions, as the appointed leaders of the household, one of us would take these assignments seriously and would succeed in ensuring what our parents requested was done. However, as we all got older and we were no longer watching whoever was youngest, assigned responsibilities weren't necessarily given; they were expected to be completed. As both my sister and mother would say, "You [are] grown and you know better!"

There were times when, as older children, no one was assigned to really be in charge; however, just based on status and age alone, we took charge. We delegated responsibilities to one another that we were supposed to do ourselves, but we used our unspoken authority to get the younger one to do it. All was fine and good at first when the older sibling was getting away with it, but once another sibling discussed what was really going on while our parents were gone, we got in trouble. It exposed our opportunities to get away with stuff and no longer do things as our parents desired them to be done. The outcome of taking charge our way definitely had more consequences when we took the opportunity to be in charge rather than be entrusted with and assigned responsibilities.

From this story, you can gather that there is a huge difference between being in charge and taking charge. There are appropriate and inappropriate times being in either position. When you are put in charge as a leader, you are entrusted with the responsibilities that come with the tasks and the decisions associated with them. As the next person in charge, you are expected to deliver on those assignments. When put in charge, you are expected to be honest about what you can do and can't do. It is a transfer of tasks that would normally be done by the parent, but is being handed to the chosen leader.

Think about babysitters and child care providers. Mrs. Jenkins, down the street, may have watched us when we were little because she was somebody's grand-mama who wanted to make a little cash on the side. It is up to the parents to make sure that Mrs. Jenkins could provide the care they desired before putting her in charge; likewise, it is up to Mrs. Jenkins to let the parents know that she isn't licensed and watching their child or children would be at their own risk. The parents probably know this already because sweet, old Mrs. Jenkins has been taking care of children for 20 years now, but she has to cover her tail. Now if Mrs. Jenkins lied about being licensed and having had all of the credentials and CPR certifications and, afterward, something unfortunate happened to a child in her care, then Mrs. Jenkins could be criminally charged. Her failure to be honest would have resulted in a potentially grave consequence.

When leaders put their colleagues or followers in charge, it is the expectation that they can do the duties, unless the colleague expresses, honestly, that they cannot. This gives the leader time to find someone who can fully perform the duties as they desire to effectively be in charge.

Taking charge can be beneficial in emergency situations. When a leader suddenly leaves with no instruction, those left behind are left to determine the best person to lead. The duties still have to be done in an informal but orderly fashion to prevent additional chaos. It is easier said than done, indeed. It takes a bold individual to take charge, to accept the responsibilities that have not been formally assigned and all that comes with it, benefits and consequences alike. Leaders who take charge, especially under such conditions, are not only admired, especially if tasks are completed, but they earn a sense of empathy because they had to pick up where situations were drastically left by the wayside. This may happen when Mommy or Daddy has an emergency and has to drop the kids off to someone at the last minute. No formal instructions are given; they drop the child off and leave. Whether it's a neighbor, grandma, auntie, whomever, the new leader is expected to immediately take charge, in hopes that the outcomes will not be detrimental. In the end, the parents are grateful for leader's last minute availability to be responsible for the task.

We do see the not-so-nice side of taking charge when the situation is emergent and all participants are aware of their roles in case of an emergency. There may be one person who wants to feel important and starts to delegate without formal assignment. An example of this is when you have older children, who pretty much fend for themselves when the parent has to roll out really quick. The older sibling automatically assumes that they are in charge and delegates the younger siblings to do this or do that. Now, how receptive do you think the younger siblings are to the older one when they didn't hear Mommy or Daddy mention who was left in charge? There will be a few raised eyebrows and extreme push back against the new law that the older sibling felt he could lie down.

The Vibe of the Household

Depending on the type of home you have can determine how much interaction you may encounter with your family in that setting. The amount of physical and social interaction is lessened in a household that has more residential space.

There may be set times of the day when the family gathers for fellowship or to discuss certain situations regarding the family unit. In the household, there is a head (or are heads) of the household who provide(s) the structure and rule setting for how the household should be run and how those who live there should function. However, the rules and regulations are not always communicated or given directly; some are told, some are implied, and some are modeled.

Many functions of a household resemble an organizational structure. This concept can be translated to how organizational structure can affect the behaviors of those who work within organizations currently. How the organization functions can determine the V.I.B.E of the employee: value, input, behavior, and emotion (morale). As we explore further, ask yourself: which domain have you created?

Apartment/Rambler-Team Design

In a rambler, all rooms are on the same floor. Family interaction occurs frequently as members pass by one room to the next. The construct of the home is horizontally linear. An organization with this construct (see Figure 1), allows the leaders and followers to work on the same level, functioning as a team. Teams can be both horizontal and vertical.[15] They may not function with the same expertise, but the input may prove essential since it is encouraged on the same organizational plane.

Figure 1. Horizontal, Linear Construct

Split Level Home - Bureaucratic Structures

A split-level home consists of 2 floors with a stairwell that separates them. In a split level home, you always know where family members are, either on the upper level or lower level, yet they do not necessarily have to interact, unless there are certain times that bring them in one place (dinner time, family time, etc.). Imagine if Mom and Dad are upstairs paying bills and discussing plans and the children are downstairs playing video games. Neither couplet interferes with the others' activities; furthermore, what Mom and Dad decide will affect the entire family with little to no input from the children.

This is an example of what occurs in some organizations. There is little to no interaction between the leaders and the followers (Figure 2).

Figure 2. Top Management Decision Making

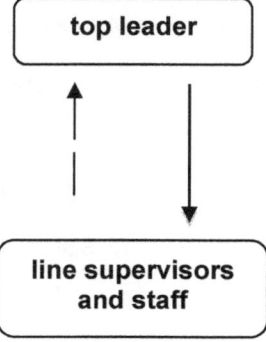

The decision making process is one-directional, solely dependent on leadership; leadership makes the decisions and instructs staff about implementation without their prior input. Communication is key in organizations when new situations or changes occur. Even though leadership makes the decisions in these matters, in order to gain buy-in or agreement and support in these efforts, the line supervisors and staff who are expected to put in the work for continued success should be kept informed in some way. Additionally, leaders should take into account the input their followers provide because they are working in the trenches or are experiencing the outcomes of their decision first hand. Allowing your followers to have input will make them feel valued and will help the leader-follower relationship grow.

Single Family Home - Networking/Stakeholder Involvement

A multi-departmental organization will have varying input toward the organization's goals; however, the work is created and completed to satisfy the goal and mission of the organization (Figure 3). With a single family home, there are multiple floors and rooms. There are entertainment areas, possible home offices, and maybe even guest rooms. There is space to accommodate the family and possibly more. Imagine the holidays and family guests are visiting. Many of the guests are in different rooms doing different things, but the overall purpose to being under one roof is for reuniting, celebration, and fellowship.

Figure 3. Multi-level Design

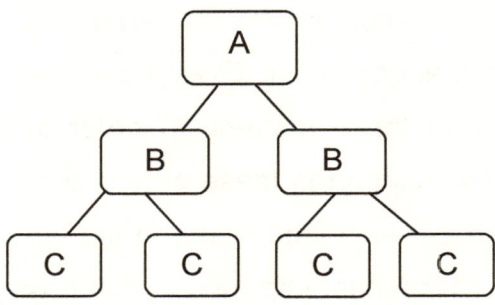

Top management (A)
Line management (B)
Staff /Stakeholders (C)

With larger organizations, top management, line management, and staff understand the mission. They work in their respective positions; however, they desire to adhere to and work toward the mission. With this type of design, stakeholders, or guests of the household, may be involved in the organization's processes and goals and provide input accordingly.

Row house/Townhouse-Functional Structure

The single-family home construct is more wide spread; however, the townhouse design has multiple areas in a more confined space. This can create a more vertically linear design of the single-family home, but is for a smaller family. This organizational design would allow other departmental input where team leaders on every level would have much of the input toward the final decisions or products. Other staff would provide input and ideas, but the ultimate decision is up to the team leads, supervisors, and top managers (Figure 4). This functional construct is efficient in situations where there are products sold and distributed quickly and at a low cost. The work gets done, but the input may not come from all parties involved if it means that the product output may be affected.[16]

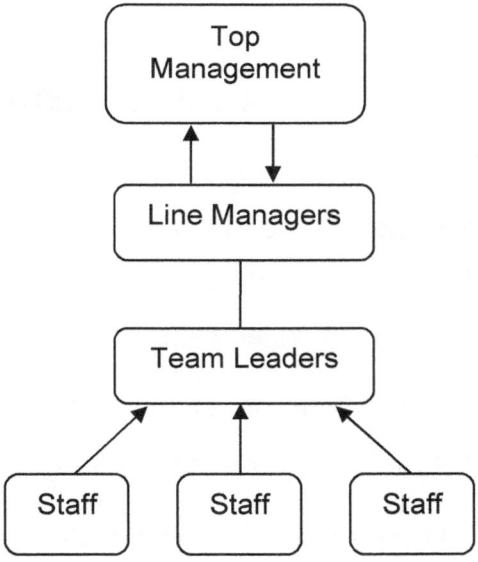

Figure 4. Vertical, Linear Construct

Employees may feel like they have worked hard to provide their contributions to the decision making process, but there is an added expectation to see some sort of follow-through once it reaches top management. If their ideas are used, they feel valued and morale is increased.

They are more willing to participate in future procedures. If employees are constantly disappointed by the final decisions, not seeing a trace of their work utilized, they may become uncooperative.

No matter what structure is used to maintain your organization, as mentioned earlier, it is extremely important to continue to establish a working and productive relationship with your followers. Ways this can be accomplished are as follows:

- Involve your followers in decision-making as much as possible.

- Trust your followers and their abilities and share the work.

- Employees can be much like family. Having a mutual understanding and a sense of trust and worth helps them grow, thrive, and succeed together.

- Be honest. Talk about issues that are challenging and work through them together.

- Create an environment where your followers want to work; limit hostile situations as much as possible.[17]

A happy family makes a happy home; happy followers support happy leaders. Create a happy work environment and a comfortable vibe in the workplace.

Leader Lessons Learned

- Know your limits as the head of your organization.

- Being in charge is an assignment; taking charge is a subjective or personal decision.

- Taking charge in emergency situations can be seen as gutsy, yet favorable.

- Tailor your leadership style based on the structure of your organization; one size does not fit all.

BECOMING THE H.P.I.C. – THE HEAD PERSON IN CHARGE

Instructions: The key to becoming the H.P.I.C. or a great leader is to know who you can count on to reach your desired goals. It is easy for you to be challenged and possibly give up, but your support network of peers, mentors, colleagues, loved ones, etc, can be there to help you through. Situations that impact your leadership not only occur in your professional career but also in your personal life. Therefore, your support system shouldn't be limited to the work environment. Document those people who you feel will provide you the support you need as you continue to excel. This chart below should serve as a constant reminder of those you trust with your future.

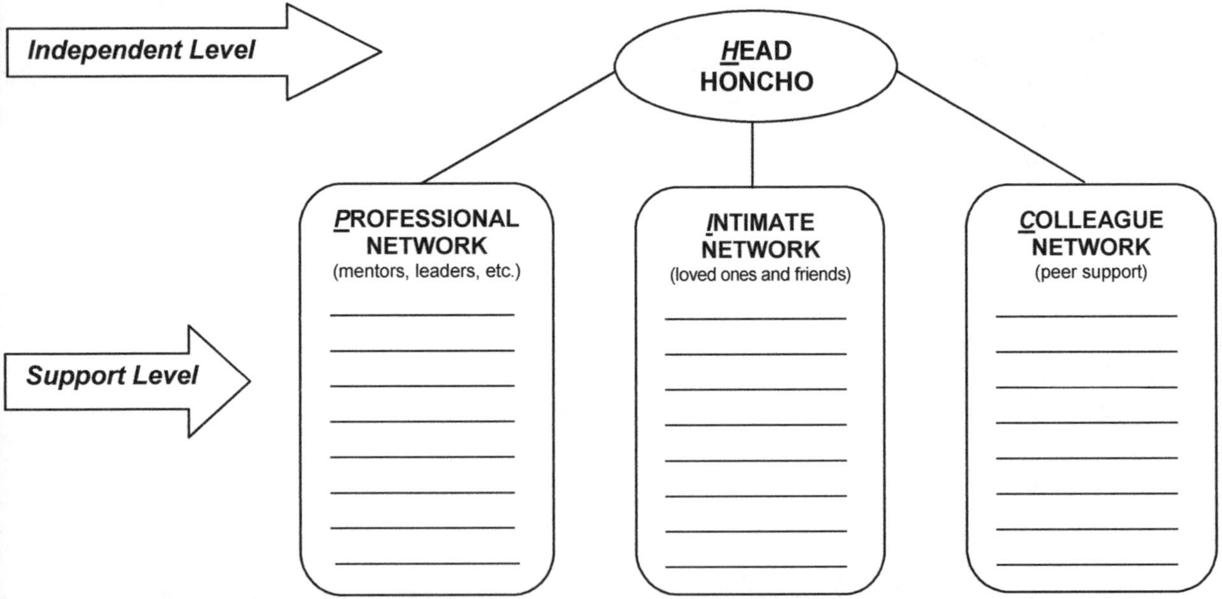

HEAD HONCHO

PROFESSIONAL NETWORK
(mentors, leaders, etc.)

INTIMATE NETWORK
(loved ones and friends)

COLLEAGUE NETWORK
(peer support)

Independent Level ↑

Support Level ↑

Chapter 4
Life of the 'Latch Key' Kid

Discovering professional independence in organizations

Latch key kids are children who reach a certain age and are lawfully able to be home alone and/or care for other children. Members of Generation X were considered the latch key kids as they grew up in a time when there were two working parents (or a single parent) in the household and the older siblings were able to take care for themselves and younger siblings in the absence of their parents.[18] I, too, have experiences as a latch key kid and it was my initial introduction into leadership and life. This is my story.

I finally turned 10 years old and earned the right to have my own key to the house. This was a proud milestone in my parents' lives when any of their children were able to gain a level of independence because of proven trustworthiness. Were there times when my parents didn't trust my judgment? Of course, but those moments were outweighed by more reassuring moments when I acted most responsibly. My parents not only entrusted me with taking care of the house when I got home and doing my homework as I was supposed to, but they also trusted me with taking care of a newborn, my little brother. Little did I know that I was being pimped, just a little bit, to save on childcare cost (however, I can appreciate that logic now). I had to pick him up as soon as I got home from school, but at that time, I was just glad that I had the opportunity to feel like an adult. My sister was allowed to work and participate in extra-curricular activities after school since I was now in charge.

I followed the same routine: pick up my brother, come in the house, change his diaper and feed him, turn on Sesame Street to let him watch it while I ate a snack and did my homework until Mommy came home (Daddy worked nights). So long as I stuck to my agenda and completed any necessary chores listed in a kind note, I was able to maintain my independence and earn opportunities for more trusted responsibilities later.

As we desire to take on positions of leadership, we have opportunities to prove our worthiness via shared experiences and talents. In high school, we work on committees and boards, serve as presidents and vice-presidents of clubs, or become team captains because we have dedicated our time over four years to get to a leadership position. We have been trusted with the function of that board, group, or club. In college, we are introduced more to the interview process that allows us the opportunity to share our experiences and how we can be a good fit for the desired position. This interview process initially proves our worthiness and gives us a chance to discuss the skill set that we plan to exhibit in our chosen careers.

We are honored to be offered an interview after foregoing a long application process, drafting paragraphs of information that showcase at least one year's experience related to the desired employment level. We become managers in stores, leaders of fraternal organizations, heads of Home Owners Associations, etc. because, at some point, we have proven to our potential followers that we should be in the seat of leadership and can do well. In these instances, we find that a certain level of education is not always the key toward success. Positive and skillful experiences can trump any degree.

We discover that some of today's business moguls and success stories are non-degree seeking or obtaining individuals. However, they still worked hard to attain (and maintain) their current success. Lack of education does not negate good, old-fashioned hard work. I worked hard for years proving to my parents that I could run their home while they were gone. I learned to cook, to clean, and to be where I was supposed to be on time due to my latch key training. This chapter takes a deeper look at how we can become trusted leaders and also gain independence when a company, organization, club, etc, is left in our hands. Are you worthy? What skills do you have? Can you learn to get to leadership independence? Let's find out!

Discovering Your Independence

In leadership, you have to be able to gauge the amount of work you can do at one particular time. Sometimes the demands of your work outweigh the capacity in which you are able to work at the time, meaning, there is more on your plate than you can handle. Stress levels can increase in fast-paced, highly critical work environments, and it is up to the leadership to ensure there is a balance between the workload and leisure. Supervisors who support their subordinates contribute to increased morale and have willing followers who want to support their leaders. However, in the leadership and corporate world, there is a circulating saying, "People don't leave jobs; they leave supervisors!" If followers have to leave, let's hope that it is on a positive note and you have contributed to their skill set so much that their desire to move on is simply because they want another opportunity to shine.

Both leaders and followers can learn to discover their independence in the workplace and continue to highlight those shining moments. Leaders can delegate duties that will help their followers grow professionally, or followers can volunteer for opportunities that will build their skill set. Either way, the undertaking of additional tasks can be a burden at times, but can be rewarding at another point in a leader's career. I have been on both sides of the fence where I learned to delegate duties as a leader and accept duties as a follower. Both situations were stressful; nevertheless, it gave me some insight into taking on more than I can handle. It also made me realize the need for effective time management skills, including advanced planning and building flexibility into my schedule.

When I worked for a local government agency, I was given the opportunity to take on the supervisory duties while my supervisor was on leave. I also had to continue to perform my own duties as well. Things were fine, at first, as I adjusted to my new role. Then, everything weighed on me all at once. Reports were due at the supervisory level, and I wasn't prepared, in advance, to meet the deadline. I had to go through impromptu training with those who were aware of these reports in order to get up to speed on report goals and deliverables. Day to day, I would go to work thinking, "Another day; another dollar!" Not a very positive attitude to have, but it kept me sane. I had two pages of things to do: one for my own job duties and one for the supervisor duties.

One morning, I woke up extremely ill and was down for a week. Not even two weeks later, I fell ill again for a few days. My doctor said that because of my lack of sleep, my immune system was compromised. Know that when it comes to your health, you must listen to your body. It is easier said than done, but if you don't pay attention to your health needs, you will suffer. I returned to work and discussed my health issue with my division chief. The outcome of that discussion was to determine what I could do on my own and when I needed to lean on my colleagues for help. Passing the baton was a tough thing for me to do as I was attached to those duties, but I have learned from this experience, and others, that if you are not healthy, you can't do anything on any list. I realized that sharing tasks helped me to not only get the work done, but also know that there are people willing to assist, if you ask and engage appropriately and have established a good sense of trust and rapport amongst your team.

I learned that delegation is not a bad thing in leadership. I used to think that some people in leadership positions overused their authority to delegate duties, but at that time and times since, I have found that it is a necessity. If the leader decides to distribute the work wealth in order to maintain good health, it can create a domino effect to the followers, provided that they are not overwhelmed due to the delegation of duties. This takes us back to the point of being able to gauge stress levels, yours and your followers. To gain that balance, there must be efforts for efficient team work and ensuring that the duties are almost evenly distributed.

As a follower who took on leadership duties, I can say that the skills I learned as an interim leader were put on my resume and helped advance me to higher positions in the government. The bottom line is this: Don't take anything learned, as a follower or leader, for granted. You never know when you will need to unlock those capabilities and use them effectively.

Unlocking Your Capabilities

"It only takes your eyes to supervise, your hands to manage, your mouth to delegate, but it takes your heart to lead." –
Dr. Janice A. Armstrong

I created the mantra above when I started my doctoral studies. After the first leadership course, I realized that having heart, more specifically, passion for what you do is motivation for you to lead others. Whether you realize it or not, the way you approach people gives them a glimpse into who you are and it helps them determine whether they have the desire to follow you or to refuse your leadership. Refusing your leadership isn't a matter of your followers being defiant, but more a matter of analyzing trust and understanding. Continue to gauge that...often. Being able to read the emotions and motives of your followers will prove beneficial and will be a lasting influence on your leadership. Body language and facial expressions can clue you into the way that you should lead your followers. It helps you to determine what is pleasing to them and what keeps them engaged. This is called having emotional intelligence. It takes practice, and is not always easily attained, but once grasped, it is a leadership skill worth developing.

As you continue to grow as a leader, you will experience those times when your greatest assets will come into play at the most unusual moments. Working under pressure will bring out capabilities that you forgot you even had, but will remember, after the fact, in less stressful situations. There was a time when I had to work "under the gun" with extreme time restraints. From that point on I knew when things had to be done at a moment's notice, I knew I had the strength to overcome the obstacle.

Some agencies host Take Your Child to Work Day (or TYCTWD), when workers are allowed to have their children shadow them during the regular workday. In some cases, the agencies have planned activities. There is usually a valuable lesson to take away from the event. I was working for a local government agency and there were plans put in place for the TYCTWD that was to occur the next day. When the TYCTWD arrived, I came into work and completed my usual routine, which involved checking my emails before getting breakfast. There was an urgent email from our supervisor stating that the original plans fell through late the day before and our team was "voluntold" (told that you are volunteering) to create activities for the children. It was 7:15 a.m. when I read this email, and the children were arriving at 9:00am! I was the only one in the office at the time, with my next colleague coming in around 7:30 or 8:00. Something had to be done, and I guess I was the one to do it.

First thing I did was panic. That's just the truth. The second thing I did was consider the ages of the children, which ranged from ages 6-16. That was a broad age range, and I had to figure out something that would engage all of them. Granted, we had about 12 children scheduled to arrive, but none of them wanted to be bored to death. I racked my brain for the initial solution and thought, "Arts and crafts." I gathered markers, newsprint, construction paper, and stickers that were in my drawer...anything that could be used for creativity. After I collected the items, I thought, "What in the world are we going to do with it?" After about 5 minutes an idea came to mind that I did, in a previous job, with my clients who needed vocational (work) assistance. It was an interactive and creative opportunity for them to determine what they desired in a job and for their lives.

In short, I changed the dynamic of an assignment that was tailored for adults and made it worthwhile for children and teenagers. We wrote visions for the future, made crafts and drew pictures related to those visions. I am a firm believer of writing the vision and making it plain so that it can be comprehended and utilized.[19] It gave the children the opportunity to truly think about their futures and what was important to them. They even worked together and supported each other on their projects, which gave them confidence when they presented the desires for their futures. It was at that moment that I realized what I truly desired in life: helping people identify what they wanted for their lives.

Helping people to determine their dreams was a process that I started when I developed a small training session about accomplishing goals in college, but never thought much of the impact on others and how much I would enjoy it. Now, I have a certification in leadership and life coaching and use my capabilities to bring this book to you. When you are entrusted with an overwhelming or time consuming task, be like Nike and *Just do it!* You never know what new skills you will build, or when you will need to use them. Continue to unlock your capabilities through valuable experiences. As you continue to grow in leadership, you will also be able to discern what skills are most appropriate for the needs of the organization you currently or will lead. Know that others are watching you and learning from you as your position as leader puts you and your capabilities in the spotlight. Remember to continue to be honest about what you can (or cannot) do, and discover the resources, knowledge, talents, abilities and skills in your followers who may be able to fulfill additional needs. Never underestimate the power of your followers, and always be open to learning from them as well. Above all, encourage your followers to continue to unlock their capabilities while providing them with opportunities to grow and lead.

The Latch Key Leader

As a leader, you now have the key of leadership in your hands. You may not be a senior, the head honcho, top executive, but that doesn't matter. Why? Anyone can gain the responsibility of a leader. A leader is one who is able to take charge of a particular situation based on the skill set necessary to complete the task or assignment. You can earn leadership by proving that you are worthy to lead or by inheriting the responsibilities in absence of the assigned leader. This can be an honor and a challenge.

There used to be a time when I was scared to lead when I worked for a former employer. There was too much finger pointing. However, the earned reward and recognition, when I did my job well, outweighed those negative moments. I survived my position by staying out of the line of fire. I always had a good work ethic from years of watching my parents' work habits. I was also taught to never burn my bridges because I might need to cross it again to obtain a referral or letter of recommendation. I grew up knowing to do well and earn good grades; once in the workforce, I learned to do well, keep a job, and earn a paycheck. There were times when I witnessed jobs not done well and paychecks were still earned, but I did not allow that to influence my ethic and in turn, ruin my reputation of a being a good worker.

As the American economy shifted and funding lessened in local government, agencies had to be creative with doing more with less. In essence, agencies had to maintain the current or increasing workload with the current or fewer employees. There was an instance where I was given the key of leadership, which unlocked my potential, more potential than I knew that I had. Due to budget cuts and doing more with less, we did not have a direct supervisor for our tasks. Our division chief entrusted us to perform the duties as assigned. My team became the "go to" staff for training needs. Just to toot our horns a little, there were no breaks in service because we were proficient and efficient.

A huge and urgent project surfaced in the agency that directly affected our department and workforce. Our division chief, with so much on her plate already, had to pass the torch to one of us. I was called into her office and asked to lead the effort, but I wasn't sure why she asked me. What in the world do I know about leading a major initiative? At the time, I thought, "What the heck is an initiative?" So I sat there trying to decide whether I should say, "Yes" or "No" to this invitation. I reluctantly said, "Yes," but explained to her that I didn't know what I was doing. She assured me that I did. I thought she was crazy to tell me what *SHE* thought *I* could do. She continued to say that I had "high potential" and she wanted to develop my skill set. I still thought, "Ok, whatever," in my head, but my mouth just smiled and said, "Thank you!" I walked out with a folder of information, along with a level of trust from my superior that this initiative thing would be completed.

This situation reminded me of my latch key days. I knew I had experience to take care of my brother, but I was entrusted to do it on my own because my parents saw that I had potential. I had to prove that I had the power: to learn, to fulfill, to execute, and to complete the duties assigned. When my division chief stated I had "high potential", she wanted to influence and guide my experiences to the next level, offering me the power that she had, but couldn't personally utilize.

To tap into my love for Hip Hop, here is another example of duty exchange. In the Hip Hop culture and history, DJing and MCing became separate tasks because the duty was passed to another individual. Initially, the DJ hyped the crowd with talent on the turntables and the verbal skills to keep the party going. As time has gone on, the DJ has focused just the music and the hype man, Master of Ceremony or MC, has gotten the party going through verbal prose or rap. The MC now had the power to do what the DJ could do, but really doesn't have to, yet the outcome of moving the crowd, was still desired. By granting me the power to lead, it did not mean that she couldn't do the work, but gave her the opportunity to delegate that power to someone else so that the outcome of the assignment could still be fulfilled.

If you are ever handed the key to leadership, what potential will it unlock? Will you be willing to take on the responsibilities that come along with accepting that key? Will you prove a level of independence and potential that will allow the previous leadership to continue to trust you with that key? If you are willing to find out how you would do in a position of leadership, use the key to unlock opportunities such as internships and networking. The key that has unlocked your responsibilities and made you aware of your skill set is the same key that will continue to unlock your potential and power. You may fear what may happen when you accept that type of responsibility, but you will continue to build a greater and stronger skill set that will make you more attractive to potential employers.

Leader Lessons Learned

- Followers trust leaders who are skilled and prove their worth.

- Unlock your capabilities in a particular area by analyzing your overall skill set.

- Know when to manage, to delegate, to supervise, and/or to lead; there is a huge difference among these skills.

- Continue to gauge and understand your roles and responsibilities and determine how they can be utilized in different capacities.

EQUALIZING YOUR LIFE

In music production, the producer and track master create a product that is kind to the ear. In order to accomplish this, they equalize the bass, treble, sound levels, etc. to ensure that the best quality sound is accomplished. All of the levels do not need to be even as a song may need more bass and less treble; however, the outcome produced should still result in satisfaction.

Below you will find areas of your life that might need equalizing because they seem a bit unbalanced. In order to make things more harmonious, you must first see where your current level is in a life area and then determine where you want to be. Use the equalizer bars to fill in your level of satisfaction in a life area, if applicable (on a scale from 1-10, 10 being the most satisfied). Fill in your bars to your current level and place a star at the desired level. You will later draft an action plan to work toward your desired results. (You can find an example in the last column. The current level is at 5, but the desired level is an 8)

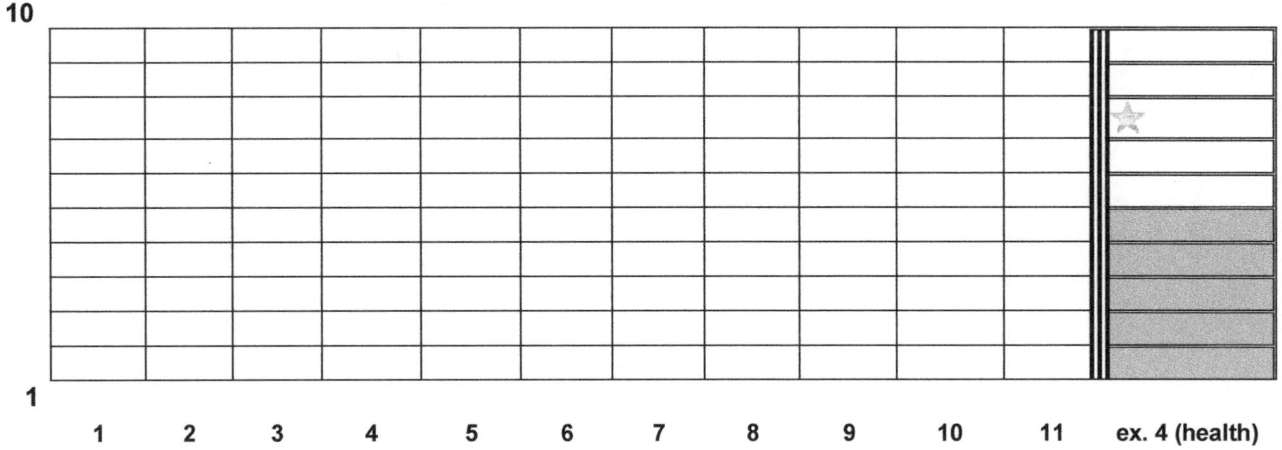

10

1

1	2	3	4	5	6	7	8	9	10	11 ex. 4 (health)

1- Work/School   2- Spiritual   3- Personal Development   4- Health   5- Leisure   6- Professional Development
7- Living Environment   8- Finances/Money   9- Family   10- Marriage/Single Life   11- Social Life

Chapter 5

Dating and Elevating

Making lasting impressions while moving into positions of leadership

There is no challenge tougher than the dating scene. I am not going to say that I didn't enjoy it. I met people and became more sociable. I got a few free meals out of the deal, and splurged on a few dates. My dating journey began when my daddy allowed me to go to my boyfriend's basketball game at the age of 15. His father picked me up, took me to the game, and brought me back home. The dating part was sitting in the backseat with my "true" love; although, he fell tired due to his game. I at least held his hand. I did go to a few dances, with friends of mine, prior to this date. It was off to the dance and back home.

Dating became more interesting, yet more complex in my college years. I had my first long-term relationship of two and a half years. It didn't last a lifetime as I thought it would have back then, but it had its joys, its pitfalls, its times of happiness, and times of heartbreak. Many lessons were learned. The next, "Oh, he is the one," came and went and the years of dating continued. Dressing to impress, being someone that I really wasn't in order to ensure that I was "his type", became quite boring after awhile.

I can't be mad at making a good first impression; the first impression was initially physical appearance for me. Is it superficial? Yes, but if you see someone that you think is attractive, I am sure that thought of "He is [or she is] fine!" occurred prior to either one of you opening your mouth to each other. I preferred tall and handsome with a great smile. I was more lenient on the tall part. The minimum requirement was that he had to at least be my height. Some of the relationships went well at first and then plummeted; others had substance, but not what I was looking for at the time. I was picky, yet, when choosing a potential mate, who wouldn't be?

There was a time when dating was not on my radar because school and other activities were priorities. This break gave me the opportunity to really think about what I truly wanted---with some or little negotiation. Prince Akeem from *Coming to America* said it well, "I want [someone] to stimulate my intellect as well as my loins!"[20] The physical appearance, yet still important, was becoming less important compared to having truly stimulating conversation of substance and meaning.

After determining my honest checklist for a potential mate, I eventually found him. Was he everything on the list? Actually, he was, once I got to know him, but I didn't make the checklist a priority at first glance or encounter. I can guarantee you that I wasn't his ideal date; I was a bit "hood" in comparison to his previous encounters. I showed up at his house in a FUBU t-shirt, jeans, and some fresh, white Nikes (I love sneakers). I was ME! As we got to know each other, we found that we possessed what we both needed. We were a great fit and offered great balance in each other's lives.

As we pursue leadership opportunities, we attend interview after interview, trying to make the greatest impression to get the ideal job. In career pursuits, with the competition being greater in this economy, the best and brightest shine. We are compared to a checklist of desires from the application process all the way to the point of hire. How can emerging and developing leaders create a good balance of experience and charisma to keep moving up the ladder of success? Continue to inquire within.

Making the First Move

So you see a man or woman who you are interested in? You are trying to determine whether you will get the person's number or just have a brief conversation to show your interest. Is asking, "How are you?" enough? Is a flirtatious look in their direction too forward? Maybe a quick compliment and a smile as you walk by will be captivating enough. You may sweat or feel nervous and even frustrated with what could possibly happen.

Some are intimidated with the potential outcome of making the first move. Previous experiences or the reputations of either the interested party or the person being sought may be questionable and might affect the process. The bottom line is that, until you try, you won't know what the actual outcome will be. You may have worried for nothing and find that either 1) the interest was mutual or 2) the person might not be your type beyond physical features.

Currently, we utilize a newer means to express interest in a potential mate that alleviates the intimidation of a face-to-face approach---the Internet and social media. In college, the first social network I was exposed to was the Internet Relay Chat (IRC). You didn't see the person as there were no pictures, no video chat; just talk via rich text. You had the choice to meet people with whom you connected, which happened in IRC groups that convened in different areas at different colleges. I met my husband via Blackplanet (www.blackplanet.com) in 2000. As mentioned before, I dated others, and though they were still nice guys, we weren't compatible or it didn't work out for various reasons. Back then, Blackplanet didn't promote their BlackLove dating site; Blackplanet was just a social network just like MySpace, Facebook, or Twitter with the initial intent of just socializing. Twelve years or more ago, it was taboo to date online. Now, it is the latest dating vehicle that has become lucrative for dating website creators and developers. The thing about online dating is that a user may find the person of their dreams or the nightmare of their lives. Social media lends itself to a person sharing the truth about him or herself and consequently, being able to lie, creating the façade of a person of whom they are not and possibly have never been. It's a risky chance you take no matter how you desire to get your mate.

Speed dating is another means that can help lessen the intimidation of approach and allows you a 15-minute (or less) glimpse into whether your interest would continue for the person or whether you shut down after 2 minutes of baggage filled ranting or self-absorbed conversation.

Whatever way you approach your potential love interest, just make sure it makes a statement. Dare to be different, meaning, be different enough to capture attention, but not so different that you are corny and a joke. Furthermore, recognize that you are not the only one in the dating arena, so you have to play the game wisely. Men, the same old playa lines aren't going to cut it; women, your attitude can be your friend or your worst enemy. Don't try to do too much too fast. Why? You don't know if he or she is really what you desire beyond looks or if YOU are even the one he or she is looking for. Information about and interaction with the person of interest may excite you. However, will he or she turn out to be the proper choice for you? Do you want to devote all of your energy into one person so early in your dating phase? Black Sheep, a rap group, said it best, "The choice is yours."[21]

The dating scene can be tiresome, and you may feel like you are being redundant in your approach. You might get discouraged and think you've exhausted all available options for a mate. Just open your mind and use additional resources, e.g. the Internet or exploring single friends of friends to broaden your scope. Whatever dating stream you choose, that first move, whether the simple salutation, the inbox note of interest, or the presentation of a phone number, still has to be made.

When pursuing new ventures, whether applying for internships, a new job, or making a new step in your life, the first move must be made. In most instances, for job or internship positions, the pursuit for the appropriate one has to occur. First moves such as exploring the Internet, participating in networking opportunities, or talking to the right people may get you where you need to be. However, twiddling your thumbs and just thinking, what you 'coulda, shoulda, or woulda" done, won't. It is totally normal to feel like you are choking when pursuing something new. It's like the lump just waits in your belly until you think, "Yes! I will go for it!" and it just surfaces into your throat, hindering your ability to breathe and be comfortable with your decision. If your interest is in a potential internship, approach your mentor or guidance counselor to ask about opportunities. If you desire a new job or position, you have to apply first to make things happen or place a call to a person of influence who can help you get your foot in the door.

When you finally make the first move, it will create insight into whether you decide to further pursue or develop that opportunity. It may not be the right time for that decision or pursuit to be made. This doesn't necessarily show failure on your part if the time isn't right. The deferment just creates another opportunity that can be explored in the future.

I remember when I started a craft business in 2004. I was hand-painting and personalizing photo albums for various occasions and organizations. I had customers who also referred friends and family to my sales site so that they could purchase items for themselves. I was excited about this new venture that initially was developed because I was a broke college student and wanted to give cheap, meaningful gifts on special occasions. As I continued to grow my business, I started to realize that my desire to do crafts was lessening. It didn't feel fun and liberating anymore; it was work! Not that it was a problem, but work is more meaningful when you can maintain your passion for it. Furthermore, there were copyright laws that did not allow me to paint and sell copyrighted material, of which were many of my designs. Unfortunately, I let it go, especially since I started going back to school and working full-time. There was not much time to dedicate to the business; I found it wasn't the right time. I didn't see this as a failure though. I was able to grow my business, learned how to develop my plan, and executed it. It was much like speed dating where I tried the business for a short amount of time and decided that I'd rather pursue something else than to move forward with something that wasn't worth the effort. Remember, nothing will be discovered or occur until a move is made. Are you willing? If so, then go, and put your best foot forward! The choice *is* yours.

First Impressions

So you are all grown up, found your independence, and understand what it takes to be, at least for yourself, a leader. How do you get others to notice your skills and your worth? How do you make yourself attractive to those interested in what you have to offer? We can go back to our years of dating to find the answers.

In our teenage years, our interest peeked for a mate who had qualities that we thought were the most ideal to us. We would create our checklist for this dime piece (or perfect 10) who we hoped to have on our arm or hold our hand. He had to be "this" tall; she had to have a nice body. He had to have straight teeth; she had to have real hair. The list can go on for decades, and essentially, it has. We have our desires and preferences for a mate who would fulfill most, many, or all of our needs. What would happen if they didn't? Then moving on would be a possible decision.

Sometimes, in the face of love, we would hang in there with a particular person who we knew was "the one," and then find out they weren't even number two. A person can try to stay in the relationship, but the chemistry may be decreasing, the personalities may clash, and that person just isn't the right fit. Where this may be the end result, it doesn't change the fact that there was something about that person, in the beginning, that made you want to try him or her out and see how it all works out. I can clearly remember times when I found guys who met the criteria, initially, only for our relationship to later crumble under the weight of being superficial. Is this the end result that we desire? No, it isn't. So we continue to pursue mates in the dating game, by making the dress to impress, "cashy-flashy", first impressions. Honestly, in the grand scheme of things, it can work. We just hope for the best.

Stereotype versus My Type

As I mentioned previously, I usually went on first dates in jeans, a t-shirt, and some sneakers. I felt that dressing up was for classy dinner occasions, and I didn't experience many of those in the dating scene until I got older. I mean, college students were broke! When I met my husband, we were both dressed down for our first few dates. At first, I really didn't fit his type; well, there were some qualities that existed, but others that were not like his other dates: petite, extremely feminine, and articulate. I was thick, rough around the edges, and spoke "Baldamorese" (the 'accent of Baltimore') with the best of them. Not that I couldn't be articulate or feminine, but I was nowhere near petite at that time. I didn't pretend well, especially if a guy didn't peak my interest.

It was a month later that I actually dressed up for him and shocked both of us. It was cold outside and I wore a skirt; my poor legs were freezing! I must have really liked this guy; my interest was definitely peaked. I showed a little leg, wore some heels and make-up to impress and had no problems doing it because I was on a mission. I wanted him to pay more attention to me. Over a month's time, he found out that I could be articulate and feminine, but honestly, with all of the façade aside, he still liked me for the person I was, not for what I was wearing even though I looked nice. I had to do what I had to do, to get what I desired. Approaching Corporate America, to me, is no different.

Corporate America has an apparent image that everyone tries to maintain. There are dress codes for men and women that are considered the norm and any deviation, in some environments, is frowned upon. I was never a business suit type of person. Dresses and skirts, especially in the winter, were the death of me. Even in blouses, button down shirts, and dress pants, I just couldn't wait to get home to strip the image, that was not me, right off of my body and return to the "Serenity of MOI." I couldn't wait for casual

Fridays. Not only was I early for work because it took less time to get dressed, but also able to get more work done because I was more comfortable. People still ask what is considered business casual for casual Fridays though. There is still debate over the dress code. However, as I continued to move into different areas of my career, I had to conform to the type of dress desired for different environments.

In some environments, wearing jeans on ANY day is a no-no, and you would get the same looks from others that you would if you worked as a stripper and decided to dance in a pink nightgown with fuzzy slippers! It's just not a good fit to the type. One thing I have convinced myself is that no matter what I wear, the intelligence that is desired in my positions is most important. Wearing jeans on Fridays has never changed the capacity of knowledge I carry to do my job. Don't get me wrong, I am not advocating that you show up to work dressed like a stripper because your mind is what matters. There are still boundaries in the workplace. Just as there are types in the workplace when it comes to appropriate dress, there are stereotypes that exist when one does not conform to the norm. This is the reason why I truly give in to meeting the standards.

It is unfortunate, at times, when attire makes the person in work environments. Honestly, it's no different than when I was in high school and it was considered lame if you didn't wear the latest gear. That's how I have felt at times. I have always worked for jobs that allowed casual Fridays, until recently. I was told that no casual Fridays existed in our department even though the agency recognizes it. The change was initially devastating, but I understood why. Our department required high visibility with senior leaders and this dress type was most desired in the work environment. I sucked it up because I wanted the job. Did I sell out? No, I just opened another door of opportunity with sacrifice. If I have to put on my clown suit to get visibility and prove my worth then I will. I am surely not going to lose a growth opportunity because of a pair of jeans. MY TYPE was not in my clothing, nor the clothing they desired me to wear. It was in my personality, my experiences, and my expertise that allowed me to continue to do my job and be recognized for it.

What I love now about wearing my casual clothing is that no one outside of work, home, school, and friendships, know what I am about. I love the shock factor of being stereotyped. I haven't changed how I talk or carry myself because that is the me I know, but when I tell someone that I have certain experiences, and they have already prejudged me, there is nothing better than seeing their faces when they discover differently.

At the turn of the millennium and as new generations entered the workforce, there has been changes from the uniformed, black suit worker. I have seen debates in professional development trainings and forums, and even on Twitter and Facebook, about whether certain dress code violations should be permitted in the workplace. However, what is interesting is that the resume has no dress code and that is the introduction that gets people in the door for interviews. Additionally, what if you only wore your "polished look" to the interview to ensure that you are taken seriously, only to be yourself when you go to work? Does the change in wardrobe negate your worth? No, it doesn't. I only know what I know and wearing a blouse is not going to throw extra knowledge in my brain, but it will allow me to be heard. What is the point of having a wealth of knowledge that no one will ever know about? So go ahead, wear the look you are expected to wear; it doesn't change who you are or what you are capable of being.

The Chosen One

We have the opportunity to exercise our right to choose the one who will lead our country every four years. What are the criteria that impact that choice? Would you make a choice without weighing the options of the matters that mean the most to you? I would hope not. The views of your candidate of choice should equate to your views. His direction for the country should be similar to your vision for the country. When your decision is made, there are things that you have determined that would give that candidate the thumbs up to get your vote.

In the dating/courting phase of life, we are faced with similar decision-making procedures. One day, the guy or lady you have been dating now wants to take your relationship to the next level. Apparently, you have made a great impression on this person of whom you have extreme interest, so of course, you, too, are ready for the next phase of your lives together. The partnership you have has either been a tremendous one or has withstood challenges, substituting them with triumph, up to this point. Bottom line, you both want to be together. You are the chosen one.

Interestingly enough, leadership is approached the same way. Think about the following as an emerging, developing, or seasoned leader: What have you mastered up to this point that makes you the one to lead efforts, initiatives, projects, clubs, organizations, or agencies? What impressions have you made that will make your followers trust that you are the one for the job? Are you influential or forgettable? When you decide to make the first move, just be sure that you are ready to impress the pants off of your leadership, so that they truly know that they chose the right one for the job!

Leader Lessons Learned

- Ambition and taking the initiative make great impressions.

- Be confident in what you have to offer to your club, organization, or agency; you'll be surprised how much confidence actually shines.

- Stand out from the crowd; the cookie cutter approach or doing the same old thing is, at times, a bore.

- Don't be afraid to fail AND succeed; both are growth opportunities.

- First impressions are lasting impressions. Make them count.

- No matter the changes you make in certain environments, reconnect with who YOU are; it's not being fake; it's being flexible.

YOU'VE GOT SKILLS!!!

Instructions: Earlier you assessed your desired goals, identified potential barriers, and decided on strategies to combat those challenging areas. For this activity, assess yourself. Why is this activity last? It is the last thing we think about. Then, why isn't it first in this book? You needed time to think more about yourself. Therefore, it should be easier to self-reflect. Self-reflection is one of the hardest things for us to do. As a leader, you have to know what makes you tick; otherwise, you won't know how effective you are or can be. In strategic planning, there is a SWOT (strengths, weaknesses, opportunities and threats) analysis done for businesses that allow owners and managers to recognize the areas which drive their successes or failures. This is an opportunity to analyze yourself! Again, in leadership, before you can assess the work of your followers, you, first, need to understand yourself.

STRENGTHS	WEAKNESSES	OPPORTUNITIES	THREATS
Ex. Ability to multi-task	*Sometimes can become overwhelming*	*Stick with the smaller items first or last depending on preference for completion*	*Choosing the right game plan to complete necessary assignments can be challenging*

Chapter 6

Taking Action- A Useful Way to Plan Your Leadership Lifestyle
(Action Plan Development)

So far, you have read how simply living your life can influence your future and desire to lead. You have answered thought-provoking questions, allowed your mental wheels to turn and have begun to determine how you want your professional life to be. Now, TAKE ACTION! In this chapter, you will explore and complete an action plan for your immediate or developing future. It will bring together what has been discussed previously. What you develop will be a living document, meaning the document is functional and subject to change, but will serve as a guide toward your success. In the leadership world, a profession called leadership coaching emerged in the late 1970's. It didn't have that particular name, initially, but the concept of being led to your desired goals have always been around. This is your opportunity to self-coach, using this action plan as your coaching tool.

Think of it this way: Let's say you desire to lose weight. There will be times when you need someone to coach you through the process of healthy eating (nutritionist), effective workouts (personal trainer), or offer some advice about physical well-being (personal trainer or physician). At any rate, when it comes time to do the actual exercising, it is all on YOU! You have to coach yourself when you are lifting that heavy weight, eating a salad instead of a burger, or running that extra half-mile on the treadmill. You have to be especially diligent about coaching yourself through the process when your support system is not around to help.

Having professional support is definitely nice, especially when you hit a wall and you no longer desire to self-motivate; the friends with whom you worked out are in the same position as you. Even while you are gaining professional assistance, coupling it with self-coaching helps you to independently reach your goals. Use this action plan to self-coach. If you feel you need the additional support, look to the support system of people you drafted earlier in the H.P.I.C. activity. If you have the money and desire to hire professional support, reach out to a trained life coach, like me, for help.

As you work further in your plan and establish your goals, ensure that they are S.M.A.R.T:

- *Specific*: Does the goal describe exactly what you want without being vague or misunderstood?

- *Measurable*: How many times will you perform said goal?
- *Attainable*: Despite the timeline, can you accomplish the goal?
- *Realistic*: Are you working within your means or abilities? Is the goal too far-fetched?
- *Timely*: is there a specific end date to your goal?

Create actions steps that will guide you toward your goal. Make sure they are specific to the goal as it is easy, with many other personal, professional, and overall life events, to be steered off task. An example of developing SMART goals and action steps exists with your action plan. Following a structured way of goal development will make the process easier and actually more enjoyable. Continue your journey, write your plan, and execute it.

Action Plan Development for Your Leadership Lifestyle

Leadership Lifestyle Goal Development Strategy

Look at your Equalizing Your Life worksheet and draft your goals based on the top four areas in which you desire to improve. Keep in mind that scores of 5 and below in an area does not indicate that you have to improve in that area, you can be content where you currently stand. You can also continue to improve in areas where you score a 6 or above as well. It's totally up to you. Identify the life development area. Write a SMART goal (or goals) for that area and action steps to accomplish the goal.

EXAMPLE:

Life Development Area #1: Health

Goal #1: Until weight loss goal is attained (TIMELY), I will exercise a minimum of three sessions per week (MEASURABLE) for the duration of at least 15 minutes per session (SPECIFIC). [It is REALISTIC and ATTAINABLE because it requires minimal and reasonable steps based on the subject]

Action Steps:

- *I will continue to follow my diet regimen.*
- *I will participate in an exercise program of choice based on the goal listed above.*
- *The potential outcome of the goal is to help me lose weight, as I desire.*
- *Call a weight loss partner for encouragement when I do not feel like exercising*

START YOUR PLAN:

<u>Life Development Area #1:</u> _____

<u>Goal #1:</u>
_____
_____

Action Steps:

1.

2.

3.

4.

<u>Goal #2:</u>
_____
_____

Action Steps:

1.

2.

3.

4.

<u>Life Development Area #2:</u> _____

<u>Goal #1:</u>
_____
_____

Action Steps:

1.

2.

3.

4.

Goal #2:
_____
_____

Action Steps:

1.

2.

3.

4.

Life Development Area #3: _____

Goal #1:
_____
_____

Action Steps:

1.

2.

3.

4.

Goal #2:
_____
_____

Action Steps:

1.

2.

3.

4.

Life Development Area #4: _____

Goal #1:
_____
_____

Action Steps:

1.

2.

3.

4.

Goal #2:
_____
_____

Action Steps:

1.

2.

3.

4.

Self-Coaching Assessment Tools

GROW Model

The GROW model, devised by Sir John Whitmore of the United Kingdom[22], is a tool used in coaching to assess and determine the correct format and direction for a coaching session.[23] Since this is an opportunity to self-coach, we will use this model to assess the development of your action plan. Here are a few questions to ask yourself:

Goals – Are your goals S.M.A.R.T based on the criteria stated earlier? Are they truly what you desire for yourself? Are you willing to work to achieve these goals?

Realistic – What does your timeline look like? Is it realistic based on the other things that are going on in your life?

Options – Who can help you reach your goals? Are there other available options if your first approach does not work?

Will – What are you willing to do in order to achieve your goals? Do you have the will to breakthrough potential barriers or try something new?

If you can answer these questions with confidence and a positive outlook on your lifestyle, then it is time to make some moves. Just be aware that all of the tools and skills you need are either already available within you or you have to capability to learn, grow, and thrive. Let the street smarts and/or life lessons you have experienced be your guide for personal and professional success. Realize that everything happens for a reason and all experiences, trials and triumphs, can be growth opportunities. Much success in your endeavors as you enhance personally and professionally.

Acknowledgments
A Million Times...Thank You!!

Special Thanks To:

- ❖ My Lord and Savior, Jesus Christ: Without you, I am nothing. Thank you for blessing my Daddy, 'Rabbitt' and my Mommy, 'Raine', with my birth and the purpose you planned for me prior to my existence.

- ❖ My loving husband, Jay: This is your book as well as mine. Thanks for the ongoing encouragement, loving words, endearing embraces and lasting support. I love you, deeply. (book cover credit: Jackie Armstrong Photography... shameless plug)

- ❖ My children, Jayson and Jaida: You give me hope to continue to succeed. I want to be a good example and I do all of this for you. I love my Suga Wugas!!

- ❖ My immediate family, extended family and wonderful friends, and sorors of $\Delta\Sigma\Theta$: Thank you for all of the text messages, emails, prayers, comments on Facebook, hugs and kisses of encouragement. It has helped me tremendously.

- ❖ My past and current coworkers, Sabine and Stacie, Cynthia, Stephen, Jerry, Candace, LaShawn, Jose, and Charlie: for reading excerpts of my papers and my book and offering your honest opinion, supporting me along the way!

- ❖ My fellow 'Bmore homey', Thomas: for helping me finalize the title of this book; it was one of the hardest things to do.

- ❖ My Regent University 2009 cohort members, advising predecessors and professors, especially Dr. Kathleen Patterson, Dr. Bramwell Osula, Dr. Sergio Matviuk and Dr. Diane Wiater: Your prayers, assistance, guidance, and the opportunity to write this book have been greatly appreciated.

- ❖ My book editor and advisors: Mrs. Yolonda Body, Mrs. Jacquelyn Gaines, Dr. David Burkus, Mrs. Natasha Beach, Mrs. Lakeisha McKnight and Dr. Tecoy Porter: thanks for your feedback via every phone call, email, or Facebook message.

- ❖ My mentors: Pastor Marion Cottrell, Dr. Robin Hailstorks, Dr. Wilson Morales, Mr. Jose Morales, Mrs. Jacquelyn Gaines, Dr. Swazette Young and Mr. Will Holmes: I want to be like all of you when I 'grow up'. You have made this journey much easier just by offering the extra push to keep me going.

- ❖ My students: I thank you for the chance to be a part of your collegiate lives and teaching me a lot as well.
- ❖ My supporters and readers: Thank you for investing in my talent and believing that this book will benefit your lives.

GOD BLESS AND THANK YOU ALL!!!

Author Biography

Dr. Janice A. Armstrong is a leadership consultant, coach, and owner of LiHK Consulting, LLC, based in the Washington, D.C. area. She received dual bachelor of art degrees in Psychology and Africana Studies from the University of Maryland Baltimore County. She furthered her education pursuing her Master of Arts degree in Counseling Psychology (Rehabilitation Track) from Towson University and pursued her Doctorate in Strategic Leadership, with a focus in Leadership Coaching, from Regent University.

Dr. Armstrong has worked for government agencies, in the Baltimore, MD and Washington, D.C. areas, in the following positions: Vocational and Educational Specialist, Training Specialist, Leadership Development Program Manager and Management Analyst. She is also an Adjunct Professor teaching courses in behavioral science. She provides a wealth of personal and professional development information that has been built over 18 years of training, professional, and organizational development experience.

Dr. Armstrong is interested in fostering professional growth and development in youth and adults. Her main focus is to teach others how to work efficiently in a multi-generational workforce. Her background in counseling psychology and leadership development fostered her love for leadership and lifestyle coaching.

Her biggest loves are God and her family. Her greatest enjoyments are spending time with family, sitting by the water, doing arts and crafts, and eating something good, tender and grilled!

Fair Use Statement

The content and activities in this book are the original creation and property of Dr. Janice Armstrong and LiHK Consulting, LLC. Use of leadership/life development activities contained in this book is granted to only the purchaser of the book. Activities should not be duplicated and disseminated separate from the book. Any additional use and/or duplication of the materials and contents will be considered illegal via the copyright laws that protect them. The writer has cited supporting tools and content and requests for use should be submitted to the respective owners of that tool.

Service Requests

To request Dr. Armstrong for speaking engagements, consultation, coaching or other related services, please submit the request, in writing, with the pertinent information (i.e. date, location, purpose, etc.) and your contact information to info@lihkleaders.com. A representative will return your request by phone or email for additional details and to discuss all business related information.

[1] "Urban Dictionary- Street Smart" http://www.urbandictionary.com/define.php?term=street%20smart

[2] Psychology Dictionary (retrieved from www.allpsych.com on 6/20/12)

[3] Maguire, J. (1990). *HopScotch, Hangman, Hot Potato, and Ha Ha Ha.* New York: Fireside Books.

[4] Lathan, S., Griffin, W., Davies, J., Combs, S. (2005), Run's House ("Camp Rev" - Season 4, Episode 406)

[5] http://www.urbandictionary.com/define.php?term=street+cred (definition paraphrased)

[6] short for "neighborhood"

[7] http://www.urbandictionary.com/define.php?term=street+cred (definition cited)

[8] http://archives.cnn.com/2001/allpolitics/07/30/clinton.office

[9] Northouse, P.G. (2007). *Leadership Theory and Practice*, 4th ed., Thousand Oaks, CA: SAGE publishing, p. 349.

[10] West, T.C. (2006), "Gender Legacies of Martin Luther King, Jr.'s Leadership". *Theology Today, 65*, p. 41-56.

[11] http://www.ethicalleadership.org/philosophies/ethical-leadership

[12] Northouse, *Leadership Theory and Practice*, 4th ed, 351.

[13] A Tribe Called Quest, "Scenario Remix" (1992), <u>The Low End Theory</u>, Jive Records.

[14] Parker, C., DeBevoise, A., Ventura, J. Reichert, J. (1984), Breakin' 2: Electric Boogaloo, TriStar Pictures.

[15] Thareja, P. (2008). Total Quality Organisation Thru 'People, Each One is Capable', *Foundry, 20*(4), July/August 2008.

[16] Miles, R.E. & Snow, C.C. (1992) Causes of Failure in Network Organizations. *California Management Review*, Summer 1992.

[17] "Importance of Employee Engagement (retrieved from http://www.managementstudyguide.com/importance-of-employee-relations.htm on 6/28/12)

[18] "Generation X: Declaring their Independence" (retrieved from http://apps.americanbar.org/lpm/lpt/articles/mgt08044.html on 6/27/12)

[19] Habukkuk 2:2 (NIV)

[20] Sheffield, D., Blaustein, B.W., and Murphy, E. (1988). "Coming to America", Paramount Pictures.

[21] Black Sheep (1988) "The Choice is Yours"

[22] "The Grow Model" (Retrieved from http://www.wishfulthinking.co.uk/2007/08/01/the-grow-coaching-model/ on 6/27/12)

[23] "The GROW Model" (Retrieved from http://changingminds.org/disciplines/hr/performance_management/grow.htm on 6/27/12)

www.ingramcontent.com/pod-product-compliance
Lightning Source LLC
Chambersburg PA
CBHW032049090426
42744CB00004B/135